Contemporary Korean Theater

Beyond Tradition and Modernization

Contemporary
Korean
Arts Series

Arts Council Korea

Contemporary Korean Theater

Beyond Tradition and Modernization

Kim Bang Ock

Hollym

Contemporary Korean Theater
Beyond Tradition and Modernization

Copyright © 2014
by Arts Council Korea

Written by Kim Bang Ock
Translated by Cho Youn Kyung, Lee Ha-young

First published in 2014
by Hollym International Corp., USA
Phone 908 353 1655   **Fax** 908 353 0255
http://www.hollym.com   **e-Mail** contact@hollym.com

Ⓛ Hollym

Published simultaneously in Korea
by Hollym Corp., Publishers, Seoul, Korea
Phone +82 2 734 5087   **Fax** +82 2 730 5149
http://www.hollym.co.kr   **e-Mail** info@hollym.co.kr

ISBN: 978-1-56591-342-4 (Hardcover)
        978-1-56591-343-1 (Soft cover)

Library of Congress Control Number: 2014950080

Printed in Korea

* This book was translated in cooperation with Ewha Research Institute for Translation
  Studies. The Romanization of Korean names and expressions in this publication follows
  the system instituted by the Ministry of Culture and Tourism of Korea in 2000.

Preface

Recent decades have witnessed remarkable progress in the quality and scale across the culture of Korean theater, the likes of which have been rare in contemporary theater outside of the West, with the possible exception of Japan. Furthermore, international exchanges in the theatrical arts have continued to expand since the 2000s. However, it is somewhat regrettable that Korean theater has remained relatively unrenowned on the international stage in comparison to those of Japan and China. In this sense, there is an encouraging sign in the decision made by the Arts Council Korea (ARKO) to publish the *Contemporary Korean Arts Series*, including three volumes on contemporary Korean theater, of which the two volumes already published—*Daehangno* by Lee Chin A, which depicts various aspects of theater in the eponymous location representative of theatrical culture in today's Korea; and *Acts and Scenes* by Kim Miy He, which summarizes works of Western play introduced to Korea in the modern age.

This book, in particular, examines Korean theater from the 1970s up to the present: a period of particular note for the partial co-existence of theatrical features from a diverse range of time periods encompassing the pre-modern, modern, and postmodern. The focus of this volume attempts to avoid overlap with Kim Miy He's work by examining original Korean plays written and staged by Koreans, as opposed to translated works. Since the 1990s, however, the boundary between original and translated plays has become blurred due to the mainstream popularization of deconstructionist trends which saw Korean performances of foreign drama defy the confines of the original text in cases, for instance, of Korean directors attempting the adaptation or reconstruction of original dramas written by William Shakespeare or Anton Chekhov.

This book opts to illustrate the narrative of contemporary Korean theater based on each decade from the 1970s to 2000s; a distinction made not for convenience of description, but in consideration of the phases of change with regard to theater or socio-cultural aspects in Korea, which shows natural demarcation by each decade. Titled *Contemporary Korean Theater: Beyond Tradition and Modernization*, this book begins its account from the 1970s, since Korean theater up until the 1960s largely revolved around the imports and imitation of modern plays from the West and representational theater centering on drama, while the 1970s began to see the establishment of its identity and development of contemporary characteristics in terms of theatrical aesthetics, which comprise a tradition that has continued to the present.[1] For the convenience of the reader's understanding, this book will firstly provide an overview of Korean theater until the 1960s and discuss contemporary Korean theater for each decade from the 1970s onward.

It was a difficult task to cover the great number of theatrical works and artists in Korea whilst providing sufficient explanations and maintaining a consistent orthographical style. In certain cases, only the playwright or the director of a particular play is mentioned depending on the context or characteristics of the theatrical work and partly since Korean theater during the subject period saw an increasing number of artists that fulfilled dual roles as both the writer and the director. Likewise, the relevant theater company was specified for certain productions and omitted for others, while the year of production premiere was either specified or omitted depending on their significance. The Korean titles of productions were translated into English in some cases to convey the same meaning in English, whereas in other cases, the Korean pronunciation was Romanized and then italicized. Productions with international recognition were written using both methods. In the case of plays whose titles were only Romanized in the Korean notation, the English meaning was included in Note as necessary, as with additional notes required for terms and expressions such as those used in traditional Korean culture. It is my sincerest hope that this book aids readers with the desire to gain a better understanding of contemporary Korean theater.

September 2014
Kim Bang Ock

Table of
Contents

01

Korean Theater Prior to the 1970s

Approaching contemporary Korean theater must begin with the distinct characteristics of theatrical history in Korea. Records in Korea indicate a variety of theatrical performances among the common people and in royal courts, which are assumed to be at least partially influenced by China and even cultures further west along the Silk Road. However, such performances failed to evolve into a coherent form of theater. Korean theatrical history shows anemic traditions in terms of dramatic literature, refined theater aesthetics, and theater architecture, which is quite different from countries not only in the West but also in the Asian region, such as Japan, China, and India, where drama or plays developed as cultural assets of high sophistication under the auspice of aristocratic classes throughout ancient and medieval ages.

In contrast, the history of traditional Korean theater evolved from the daily lives of the common people, comprised of simple folklore-based performances developed around the 18th century, such as *talchum* and *pansori*. Although *talchum* is claimed by some to have been transmitted from similar mask performances abroad or influenced by Buddhist culture, its origin specifically traces back to folk performances staged as part of the culture among agrarian communities in Korea up to the 20th century. *Talchum* is a performance in which performers adorn masks and vibrant costumes to portray characters and dance to the accompaniment of various musical instruments, featuring a progression of simple spoken lines and movements. The performance starts with *gilnori* or *apnori*,[2] in which the performers introduce themselves in a short parade to rouse excitement among the audience, and ends with *dwitpuri*, a celebratory dance featuring all of the performers and willing members of the audience as well. The main performance consists of eight to ten short episodes conveying ritualistic scenes of equivocal meaning, and scenes featuring themes such as scathing satire on the *yangban*[3] class, in relation to social landscape and conflicts that were prevalent in the 18th and 19th centuries. *Pansori* is defined as a solo performance narrative song, in which the singer leads an epic story with song, spoken lines and simple movement, in line with the rhythm of *buk*[4] played by the *gosu*.[5] The story in such performances generally derives from the joys and sorrows of the common people that pervade oral literature or folktale. Unlike *talchum*, which primarily served as agrarian entertainment, *pansori* was loved by the rich and the aristocracy and developed into a form of intricate artistry by the early 20th century. Other traditional performing arts, of unknown origins and close connections to the lives of commoners, include the shamanic ritual of *gut*, and *gutnori*, the theater-form entertainment performed as part of the *gut* ritual, which have developed to take on different features according to each region. They have also served as a source of inspiration for performing artists in contemporary Korea through a wide range of mythical elements, songs, dances, musical performances, symbolic costumes, and props.

As was the case in Japan and China, real theater culture in the Western sense began in Korea towards the end of the 19th century with the political pressure from the modern forces of the West, and the aspiration and curiosity of intellectuals toward Western modernism. Having achieved modernization relatively early through the Meiji Restoration, the late 19th century saw Japan expanding its influence over Korea with the eventual aim of projecting power to the continent, which resulted in the annexation of Korea to the Japanese Empire in 1910. The Japanese colonial occupation continued for 36 years and resulted in overlapping with the process of modernization in Korea. Although moderate differences exist regarding the specific period, theatrical culture in the Western sense is largely agreed to have begun around 1908, with the indoor staging of the *changgeuk*[6] titled *Eunsegye* (*The Silver World*). Subsequent years witnessed the imitation and localization of early-modern *shimpa* theater[7] from Japan, whereas from the 1920s onwards, Korean intellectuals that had studied in Japan during the occupation began to introduce and imitate modern

1 *Talchum*
2 *Pansori*
3 *Gut*
(Photo © Yonhap News)

forms of theater, in particular, realistic dramas and performance styles. However, modern Western and realist theater as studied and imported from Japan by prominent figures such as Hyeon Cheol, Kim Woo-jin, Hong Hae-seong, and Yu Chi-jin are considered somewhat inauthentic from the present perspective because their productions generally failed to surpass the simplistic level of proclaiming enlightening morals or sentimental impressions, while pioneers in Korean theater sought realism through their passionate composition and performance of dramas focusing on modern identity, resistance to Japanese aggression, and poverty under colonial rule. This period also tentatively introduced the translation and performances of dramas by Western authors such as William Shakespeare and Henrik Ibsen, as well as German expressionist dramas.

In 1945, Korea was liberated upon Japan's defeat at the end of World War II. Although theatrical circles began to dream of reviving the art form and made efforts such as the establishment of the Drama Company of the National Theater of Korea, the subsequent origination of the Korean War (1950-1953) proved a significant setback. An overview of the period from liberation to the 1950s shows the penning of realism-based dramas dealing with the chaotic aftermath of liberation and the scars of war amid the prevailing trend of pre-modern popular dramas, such as *shimpa* and women's *changgeuk*. Significant playwrights during this time include Kim Yeong-su, whose 1948 play *Hyeolmaek* (*Kinship*) offers a naturalist depiction of poverty in the slums after liberation; O Yeong-jin, whose witty prose in his 1949 work *Still Living President Lee Jung-saeng* satirized the greed of pro-Japanese collaborators after the liberation; and Yu Chi-jin, who had been actively engaged in theatrical activities during the occupation and went on to write *I Want to Be a Human, Too* and *The Han River Flows*, which offer a somewhat melodramatic view of the desolate lives before and after the war, from the anti-communist perspective.

Economic hardship after the Korean War and political instability caused by national division led to the April 19 Student Revolution in 1960 and the May 16 Military Coup in 1961. Despite the yoke of military dictatorship, however, the Korean economy began to see gradual growth and meaningful movements were identified in the cultural world. The 1960s saw the establishment of small-scale theater companies, or coterie theaters, many of which served to lay the foundation

Hyeolmaek directed by Lim Yeong-woong, 1998 (Photo © National Theater of Korea)

for Korean theater in the present day, including Shilhum Theater Group (*shilhum*, also spelled as *silheom*, meaning "experiment"), Jayu Theater Company (*jayu*, meaning "freedom"), and Minjung Theatre Company (*minjung*, meaning "the people"). Born out of the effort to overcome the deep wound of the war, Korean culture in the 1960s was largely stimulated by American culture under the influence of the U.S. military government in Korea, while literature and movies were influenced by the trend of modernism prevailing in post-war Europe, such as existential nihilism or Theater of the Absurd. Furthermore, practitioners in the theatrical arts also diversified away from the propensity for realism and began to introduce a variety of modern dramatic styles, adopting not only realistic but also non-realistic styles from Europe and the U.S. The plays introduced during this period include those of Eugène Ionesco, Samuel Beckett, and Edward Albee, as well as the dramas of Tennessee

Williams, Arthur Miller, and Eugene O'Neill, along with a vague importation of Konstantin Stanislavski's psychological realism in acting which came to Korea through the U.S. and Japan.

The standards of original theater became heightened during this period, while realistic dramas had entered a phase of stability and continued to be published alongside works of eclectic realism by writers, such as Park Jo-yeol and Lee Geun-sam, whose influences included Theater of the Absurd and epic theater from abroad. Park Jo-yeol's dramas, *A Dialogue between Two Long-necked Men*, *Tourist Zone*, and *Rabbit and Hunter*, presented sophistication in describing the painful reality of national division with his unique allegory and modern sense. Meanwhile, Lee Geun-sam satirized the zeitgeist amid the emergence of materialism in society, using expressionist and epic theatrical methods in *Manuscript Paper* and *You Do Get Some*.

Following in the footsteps of Yu Chi-jin's realist dramas on agrarian communities before liberation, a number of playwrights published dramas which describe poverty in rural areas and devastation caused by the war, including Cha Beom-seok's *Sanbul* (Forest Fire), Cheon Seung-se's *Manseon* (Full Ship), and Roh Gyeong-sik's *Daljip*[8] (Straw Heap). Cha Beom-seok's *Forest Fire* (1962) convincingly depicts the story of a family and a young couple in a village deep in the mountains, who are powerless in the face of utter destruction between the forces of North and South Korea as opposing ideologies clash during the Korean War. *Full Ship* (1964) employs outstanding character portrayal and well-founded composition to present the wretched reality of a fisherman's family whose poverty forces them to venture out to the storm-stricken sea, only to become stranded after attempting to catch an excessive amount of fish. *Straw Heap* (1971) is a memorable character illustration of a strong-willed old woman in the countryside who refuses to despair despite losing her beloved son and hope through the Korean War. These remarkable works of realist drama indicate that Korean dramatic literature developed into a mature art form during the 1960s. Although a wide range of plays from Korea and abroad was introduced and staged, with various trends including Western Theater of the Absurd, Korean eclectic realism and realism, performances were limited to a few theaters, including Korea's only proscenium stage at the time in the Myeongdong National Theater (present-day Myeongdong Theater), the Drama Center, which had reopened with an innovative design, and a few small-scale theaters with less than 100 seats, quite often without concept or firm basis in terms of direction or staging techniques. Furthermore, the penetration of competing media, mainly movies and television, deprived the theater not only of its audience but also talented performers, which added to the difficulties facing theater practitioners and their dream of developing the theatrical art.

1 *Sanbul* directed by Lee Jin-soon, 1962
2 *Manseon* directed by Choi Hyun-min, 1964
3 *Daljip* directed by Lim Yeong-woong, 1971
(Photo © National Theater of Korea)

02

Modernization of Tradition and Introduction of Western Experimental Theater in the 1970s

As industrialization and export growth of the 1970s began to grow the economy under President Park Chung-hee's Third Republic, Korean society in general started to demonstrate greater public interest in culture, and the number of theater companies and performances increased, as did the number of theaters. The National Theater of Korea was constructed near Mt. Namsan in 1973 and the Korean Culture and Arts Foundation was launched in 1974, as the first steps towards providing systematic support to artists. If the 1960s had revolved around translated plays, a variety of original plays were presented in the 1970s and the Korean Theater Festival was founded in 1977 with the aim to promote original plays.

Despite the mixed coexistence of a variety of formats, theater until the 1960s was characterized through literary theater based on dramas and the influence of modern theater from Western countries. Entering the 1970s, however, Korean plays began to gain greater awareness in terms of identity and showed signs of escaping the uniformity of drama-based representational theater to the intense theatricality of non-representational theater with the emphasis on performance.

The recovery of interest in traditional performing arts, combined with intense curiosity towards Western non-representational theater, generated a sensational wave of new theatricality; under the ideologies of nationalism and populism, traditional performing arts became a means of restoring identity and opposing dictatorial rule.

Modernization of tradition is a recurring theme for contemporary theater in Korea. As mentioned earlier, traditional Korean performing arts are limited to a few forms including *talchum*, *pansori*, and *gut*. Nevertheless, theatrical practitioners in Korea are second to none in Asia in terms of pride towards the legacy of traditional performing arts, which serves as a ceaseless source of creative inspiration. During the imperial occupation, Japan attempted to exterminate traditional Korean performing arts for political purposes, which resulted in the extinction of the lineage of *talchum* as an art form among agrarian communities. Regardless, the 36 years under Japanese rule failed to extinguish popular love for the *pansori*, and such forms of traditional performance have since transformed to a modernized form: *talchum* has turned into *madanggeuk* (yard performance) and *pansori* into *changgeuk*. Strictly speaking, Western modern theater based on logical dramas and proscenium stages—in particular, representational theater focusing on realism—had indeed a dominant influence on Korean public and theatrical culture, but only for a few decades in Korea's long history, and the form of drama remains familiar to the audience simply through present-day television soap operas.[9] As Western modern theater was introduced during the humiliating period of Japanese rule and cultural influence from the West originated from the process of imperialistic expansion and exploitation, intellectuals in Asian countries including Korea viewed nationalism as an inevitable connection to modernization. Having endured the Japanese invasion, the intervention of world powers following the Korean War, and the oppression of military dictatorships, Koreans rediscovered traditional arts as the most familiar mechanism for resistance and a repository of possibilities, which provided a new alternative for future developments in the arts. In this respect, although it is truly important to preserve and transmit traditional arts, such art forms must also adapt and modernize to meet the demands of the time. Therefore, the implicit emphasis on being rooted in Korean tradition was a kind of shibboleth prevalent among artists in any given period claiming to be true to the Korean legacy. The modernization of tradition was a topic of obsession for contemporary theatrical performers who were sometimes motivated by the desire for recognition in the West, which was the cultural "Other." These aspirations were interlinked with interculturalism in the 1970s to 1990s and global cultural exchange since the 2000s, leading up to the present day.

In the 1970s, modernization of Korean tradition progressed from different starting points and arrived to similar points.

The first starting point is the widespread interest in traditional performing arts and folklore across society. The Park Chung-hee government pushed ahead with economic development and nationalism and launched government-led cultural activities including folklore competitions and designation of important intangible cultural heritages, which ignited the interest in traditional performing arts across the academic and cultural domains. The second is the nationalist movement and the fight against dictatorship led by university students. Nationalism served as a means for the authoritarian regime to govern the country, and at the same time, as a political and cultural ideology for university students to resist the Park Chung-hee regime. The third is the effort to modernize tradition carried out by coterie theater companies, mainly led by playwright Yun Dae-seong and director Heo Kyu, under whose leadership the Theater Group Minye (*minye*, meaning "folk arts") played a pivotal role in this movement. Forth, theatrical practitioners, who studied abroad in the U.S. and were influenced by experimental theater popular at the time in the West, brought a passion for experimental theater to the Drama Center, which resulted in the cultural encounter with Korean tradition. Above all, the strongest and most continuous impact in terms of theatrical art originated from the experimental theater mainly staged by the Drama Center. Naturally, this is not to imply that theatrical forms in the 1970s were merely limited to modernized version of traditional and experimental dramas. Dramas based on eclectic realism or non-realism persevered through the 1960s to continue to be published throughout the 1970s. In particular, leading playwrights in the 1970s, such as Choi In-hoon, Lee Hyeon-hwa, and Lee Gang-baek published outstanding pieces of drama whose standard has rarely been matched since.

Yu Deok-hyeong: A Pioneer of Contemporary Korean Theater at Drama Center

The Drama Center was established in 1962 as a modern, sophisticated venue for the performing arts with financial backing from the Rockefeller Foundation, under the leadership of Yu Chi-jin, a pioneer in Korean theater since before Korea's liberation from Japanese colonial rule in 1945. The center featured a semicircular auditorium with 470 seats, surrounding and overlooking a proscenium arch and a thrust stage, which allowed actors and actresses to perform or appear and disappear behind the seats or aisles. The venue was a cutting-edge theater of considerable rarity worldwide at the time, not only for the highly advanced lighting and sound systems, but also for eliciting design strengths from iconic theaters across all times, such as the outdoor theater and proscenium stage from Ancient Greece, Shakespearean stage design, traversable passages found in *kabuki* theater.

Perhaps due to the overtly advanced sense of space,[10] the center had not produced remarkable results in the 1960s and it was during the 1970s that the venue served as a birthplace for Korean experimental theater. Over this period, directors Yu Deok-hyeong and Ahn Min-soo returned from studying in the U.S. and started to stage new forms of productions centering on the Drama Center under the influence of Western experimental theater prevalent at the time. Yu Deok-hyeong, who was in fact the eldest son of Yu Chi-jin, returned home from studying stage lighting at Trinity College and Yale University Graduate School in the U.S. and hosted a directorial workshop at the center in 1969. Presenting several scenes selected from dramas by young writers, his performance was notable for the bold attempt to veer away from the original text. During the show, muscular men would demonstrate synchronized movement in mime, martial arts, and dance, when a performer suddenly descended from above by rope; stage devices in abstract forms made of iron bars were made to move with wheels attached; and intense illumination would create a striking contrast of light and shadow. At the time, Yu's creative use of staging effects came as a shock to theatrical circles, which were predominantly based on representational staging.

A later production by Yu Deok-hyeong in 1973, *Chobun*[11] (*The Straw-thatched Grave*) served as a milestone and paved the way for contemporary theater in Korea. An adaptation of Oh Tae-suk's drama featuring a death and the consequent funeral on an isolated island and the ensuing conflict between the primal order among the islanders and the laws of the external society, Yu Deok-hyeong invoked a ritualistic setting suggestive of Antonin Artaud or Jerzy Grotowski and overwhelmed the audience in portraying the pained movements expressed on the dark, netted stage by actors unclothed from the waist up; the rhythms created from such movements; language disintegrated and reconstructed into sound; and audacious lighting techniques reminiscent of abstract paintings. Yu Deok-hyeong directed a total of seven works. Whereas those from his early years showed abstract and inscrutable aspects in terms of visual movements and images, those in his later years delved into moments of suspension, slowness, and silence.

His 1980 production of *When Spring Comes to Hills and Fields* (written by Choi In-hoon), the story of a leper's family living in seclusion told in a folktale format, featured the maximization of slow movement, painstakingly deliberate and restrained language, and a sense of tension created by the pauses and silence between performers, which allowed the audience to experience new sensations with regards to time and space. His last production in 1981 was *Sanssitgim*[12] (written by Lee Hyeon-hwa), the story of a woman who is forced to seek help at an isolated house after a tire is punctured on her car, only to become the sacrificial victim of an unknown ritual, which started with an atmosphere of relative realism and unfolded into the shocking process of the woman's metamorphosis into an entirely different entity in the spiritual and physical sense, through an intricate shamanic process resembling *ssitgim-gut*, a ritual for cleansing spiritual grievances and guiding spirits to the underworld.

Whereas Korean theater applied its representational inclination even to Theater of the Absurd, Yu Deok-hyeong was the first director to offer aesthetic originality in terms of staging, which allowed theatricality to be experienced as a performance as opposed to being subordinate to the drama. Even so, he did not simply imitate Western experimental theater. Just as the famed artists of Western experimental theater such as Artaud, Grotowski, and Brecht were inspired by traditional plays from Asia, Yu Deok-hyeong strived to find the base of his experimental productions in Korean or Asian traditions of entertainment performances with particular interest in unique Korean legacies, including funeral rites, shamanic rituals, and folktales; and devoted himself to the endeavor of finding authentic Korean rhythms by training both the mind and the body through *talchum*, *hapkido*, *karate*, and *kenjutsu*. In 1974, *Chobun* was invited by La MaMa Experimental Theater to be staged in New York and went on to receive positive reviews.

Ahn Min-soo: Encounter of Traditional Asian Theater and Theater of Cruelty

Ahn Min-soo had originally pursued a career as an actor, later completing postgraduate studies at the University of Hawaii in the U.S. In those years, the Kennedy Theatre at the University of Hawaii at Manoa served as a bridge between Eastern and Western theater, through which Asian countries intended to introduce their own traditional theater and Western theatrical practitioners could satiate their keen interest in traditional Asian theater. Ahn Min-soo was shocked as he first encountered the refined and stylized forms of traditional Asian theater, including *kabuki*, *noh*, and Beijing opera. After returning home, he took the lead in staging experimental theater at the Drama Center in the 1970s, along with Yu Deok-hyeong. He strived to embody the excruciating pain caused by the cruel and absurd aspects of life through the spectacle of total theater with a powerful expression of cruelty, selectively and eclectically absorbing facets of traditional Asian theater to create a vibrant and sophisticated stage. Unlike Yu Deok-hyeong, who was engrossed in staging abstruse visual performances surpassing the original text, Ahn digested the text with meticulous analysis and imbued minimum degrees of probability and logic to characters and plots, thereby allowing the audience to easily understand his productions, and pursuing strong staging effects.

His 1974 production of *Tae* (*Lifecord*, written by Oh Tae-suk) is derived from the tragic historical event in which King Sejo (r. 1455-1468) dethroned his nephew and previous king Danjong (r. 1452-1455), killing him as well as loyal families faithful to him. Instead of strict adherence to historicity, Ahn Min-soo interpreted this work to underscore universal themes, such as mankind's barbarity and tenacious attachment to life, which was symbolized as *tae*, the Korean term denoting the organs dedicated to a fetus during pregnancy. Amidst the scene of the previous king's retainers being hung up like meat at the butcher's and tortured with their screams made all the more grotesque by the red illumination, the horror is punctuated by the screech of a newborn baby, followed by a long, white scroll naming those who are condemned to death, providing a sharp contrast with the imagery of the long, red umbilical cord traversing the stage. During the scene of King Danjong's assassination, the audience was met with the sound effect of ambulance sirens and the rattling of machine guns to symbolize the dictatorship of that time.

The 1976 production of *Hamyeoltaeja*, whose title is a transliteration of the eponymous "Hamlet" using Chinese characters of similar pronunciation, was the first Korean adaptation of Shakespeare's original *Hamlet*. The scenes generally followed the overall frame of the original storyline in this adaptation, but with the dialogue condensed into one sixth of the initial script, instead offering metrical Korean poetry and attempting to convey greater emotional substance within the abridged content. As was the same with the original work, Hamlet was troubled by the ugliness of the world and the frivolity of life. However, the adaptation was set in ancient Korea, featuring characters of Korean names and backgrounds; conflicts were simplified by removing characters such as Fortinbras, Guildenstern, and Rosencrantz; female characters of Queen Gertrude and Ophelia were defined as being quiet and submissive Korean women; and the performance was flavored with the overall atmosphere of meditation and salvation. Ahn's interpretation was completely different from the dialogue-centered Shakespeare productions of the West in that his production featured slow and restrained

Tae directed by Ahn Min-soo, 1974 (reproduced in 2000 by Oh Tae-suk)
(Photo © National Theater of Korea)

rhythms and extremely patterned motions. To create such distinctions, Ahn trained performers to focus on mediation, breathing, and traditional physical training techniques, and studied distinct rhythms emanating from motion within cessation. Unique aspects of his staging include white makeup to cover the performers' faces as in Beijing opera; the notion that Ophelia is not sent to a nunnery but rather made to pound a Dharma drum in agonizing contemplation at a Buddhist temple; and the exaggerated movements in the duel scenes reminiscent of Japanese samurai. Despite its outstanding quality, *Hamyeoltaeja* was swayed by the nationalist sentiments prevalent in Korean theater at the time, generating the criticism that it drew considerable influences from foreign theatrical modes such as *kabuki, noh,* and Beijing opera. Ahn personally conceded that Korean folk theater was too spontaneous and simple, and insufficient in terms of typical formality to depict the graceful beauty in the tragedy of *Hamlet*.[13] This production was also staged abroad upon invitation from the U.S. and across Europe, for which Ahn intentionally emphasized traditional elements such as *jeongak,*[14] *sijo,*[15] and *talchum*. His 1980 production, *Chohon* (*Invocation of the Dead*) sent another shockwave through Korean theater as it proceeded for two hours and a half with the entire performance consisting of 14 women in white mourning clothes whose sole acts are to *gok,*[16] or wail in sorrow, while bowing and prostrating, without specifying any settings in terms of the story or characters. Up to the 1980s, Ahn Min-soo had staged a total of eight productions and ended his staging career with early retirement.

Oh Tae-suk: Molière Revived in the Traditional Korean Performing Arts

Unlike Yu Deok-hyeong and Ahn Min-soo, Oh Tae-suk had never studied abroad, having instead started theatrical activities at university in the late 1960s by publishing dramas considered to be works of abstruse modernism or the Theater of the Absurd. The subtle openness and spontaneity are characteristics of Oh's plays and commensurate to the trend among universities at the time to rekindle awareness towards traditional performing arts, which is likely to have aided this playwright and director's outstanding sensibilities to surpass the representational and logical nature of Western theater. Having joined the Drama Center, Oh spent the 1970s collaborating with Yu and Ahn, and his production *Soettugi Nori* was staged in 1972 at the Drama Center to become a meaningful performance not only to him personally but also to the center.

Soettugi Nori is a reconstruction in the form of a traditional Korean performing art, adapted from Molière's *Les Fouberies de Scapin* (*Scapin's Deceits*). Almost the entire script was rewritten, except for the general synopsis and characters borrowed from the original work, and the adaptation made active use of traditional Korean elements, such as *talchum*, *pansori*, and puppetry. It is widely told that Oh Tae-suk's theater features omissions, leaps, and meta-fictional wit, so even when depicting the pain and scars of life, his plays never abandon the element of liveliness and laughter. If Yu Deok-hyeong and Ahn Min-soo presented avant-garde productions with abstruse, heavy, and serious theatrical atmospheres while borrowing from the sensibilities of traditional performing arts, the Molière adaptation *Soettugi Nori* presents a farce filled with gaiety, both vibrant and somewhat satirical. The resulting production was an energetic performance in which the farcical vivacity of the original meets the vigor and open format of *talchum* to create incessant movements and transitions. In particular, the three-dimensional and structurally open design of the Drama Center stage was employed to the full effect to allow for frequent scene changes and flexible stage entrances and exits, as well as the usage of various stage props such as a round straw mat, resembling the traditional set-up for *talchum* consisting of a swing and a slide over a straw mat, along with ropes running from the ceiling, and access holes built under the auditorium. As in the traditional *talchum* and *pansori*, director Oh sat down on the straw mat and led the performance while playing a drum, and characters in exaggerated costumes to appear tall or fat moved and danced to the traditional *talchum* rhythms. Such intrinsic traits of the farce are commonly shared across traditional Korean theater including *talchum* and puppetry, and aptly complement Oh's artistic disposition.

In the 1970s, Oh Tae-suk engaged in works outside of the Drama Center, and major productions of this period included *Transplant Surgery* (1971), inspired by the motif from traditional puppet shows; *A Medicine Seller* (1973), which recounts the story of a medicine seller wandering around to sell his wares by offering simple entertainment and wordplay, which follows the traditional solo-narrative performance of *pansori* by featuring two performers including an actor and an actor-percussionist; and *Chunpung's Wife* (1977), which depicts the Korean viewpoint on life and death as easily traversable states, inspired by a classical novel of a heroine wandering in search of her cheating husband, and by the mask dance *miyalhalmi*, in which an ailing elderly woman also roams to search for her husband. Even his early modernist works with absurdist leanings evoked an unfathomable atmosphere without logic, rather than the philosophical reasoning in proximity to the Theater of the Absurd. In *Chunpung's Wife*, for example, this tendency is liberated from all hindrances. The play features a liberal mixture of several themes prevalent in traditional literature—life, death, and reincarnation; man and woman; resentment and humor; obsession and detachment. Rather, it is more appropriate to suggest that such elements are

Chunpung's Wife directed by Oh Tae-suk, 1977 (Photo © Mokwha Repertory Company)

dissolved within Oh's unique sensibilities as opposed to being mixed among themselves. *Chunpung's Wife* transcends the boundary between the dead and the living, man and woman, and presents a space of unbridled entertainment, which is also the theme of this work.

A Medicine Seller shows tints of modernism in the aspect of wandering around in search of one's identity, but also suggests that peddling medicine serves as entertainment and a shamanic ritual and is rooted in the marketplace as a venue of livelihood. Oh Tae-suk's drama succeeds in overcoming the Western dichotomy between work and play, life and festivity. It is not a counter-logical world appearing in the Western Theater of the Absurd, but a realm of non-logic and transcendental logic that surpasses logic entirely from the very beginning, which is generally called "*nori* (play)" or "*nori jeongsin* (spirit of play)" by Koreans. It is a non-logical venue, a venue for life, a venue for encountering cosmic energy and merging life and arts, and where content and form are harmonized to the point where the form equates to the content, and to play equates to the message itself. Theater as entertainment is the polar opposite of theater as a representation of life, which is a notion proposed by Western rationalism. Critiques towards Oh Tae-suk's theater, however, had already begun at the time, chiefly that Oh's apparent obsession with visual aspects or the abundance of visual elements tends to distract the audience from understanding his theater.

Oh Tae-suk has remained active to the present day since establishing his own theater company in the 1980s and forming his unique theatrical world, but his productions in the 1970s are often mentioned together with those of Yu Deok-hyeong and Ahn Min-soo of the Drama Center for their shared characteristics. Drama critic Kim Suk-hyeon identifies the common aspects of the three artists as the essential view of life as absurd suffering, which is based on their shared childhood experience of the horrors of war; their endeavor to escape the realist representation customary in theater up to the 1960s by presenting a non-representational and complete production; and their contribution to the modernization of Korean tradition through interculturalism.[17]

Succession of Traditional Performing Arts
as Political Satire

From the late 1960s, modernization of traditional theater became a propositional theme for the political theater movement mainly led by university students. Under Park Chung-hee's presidency, Korea achieved rapid economic growth at the cost of freedom under suppression by the military dictatorship, which led to the gradual emergence of resistance from students and intellectual groups. University students actively engaged since the early 1960s in the movement to preserve and transmit traditional performing arts, a part of which resulted in the organization of Talchum Research Society led by Kim Ji-ha and Jo Dong-il, to study and restore *talchum*, the traditional mask dance. *Jinogwi-gut*,[18] or *The Underworld Entry Ritual*, written and staged in 1973 by Kim Ji-ha, was considered the first *madanggeuk*, featuring narration expressed in *pansori*, and vivacious entertainment combining the rhythms of *talchum* and poetic dialogue. The premise of the play features three goblins as the primary antagonists tormenting innocent farmers,[19] the goblin of foreign crops (*oegokgwi*), the goblin of floods (*suhaegwi*), and the goblin of tenant farming (*sononggwi*), while the narrative depicts the strong determination of the farmers to resist the goblins and the eventual sense of victory. The performance starts as the narrator uses *pansori* to describe the stark reality facing rural communities, after which the three goblins enter the stage while wearing ridiculous masks and engaging in *talchum*, to be defeated by the farmers eventually after dramatic confrontations and struggles. The scenes are punctuated by intervals with dance routines, the last of which, *dwitpuri* (a wrap-up festivity), presents the scene of a political protest. *Jinogwi-gut* was premiered in a church; however, the play was originally written with the purpose of rural enlightenment, and stage production elements were entirely excluded, such as stage devices, lighting, costume, and intervals between acts or chapters, in order to enable the production to visit rural areas or relevant sites and stage the performance with ease.

As for *madanggeuk*, "*madang*" literally refers to the front or back yard in a traditional Korean house, which served as a multi-purpose space used for housework, farming, entertaining guests, and rest, whereas "*geuk*" simply refers to a work of theater. In addition to the concept of space, "*madang*" in *madanggeuk* bears other meanings. First of all, if it can be said that the Western modern play is performed indoors with clear demarcation between the stage and the audience, *madanggeuk* takes place outdoors as a performing space where performers and audience meet without boundary. A specialist in the theoretical study of *madanggeuk*, Im Jin-taek explains that central to the medium is the idea that the performance and the audience form a whole, and by extension, the audience is the master of the play; and therefore, the encounter between

Madanggeuk (Photo © Yonhap News)

the performance and audience symbolizes equality, openness, collectivism, and participation. Furthermore, as the boundary of "*madang*" is not defined, the stage is created naturally once the audience surrounds the performers, and therefore, this spatial concept is fluid and variable in nature.[20]

Madanggeuk in the 1970s are categorized as follows: plays that actively utilizes the structure and forms of *talchum*, such as *Sori-gut Agu*, *Miyal*, and *Ssitgimtal-gut*; plays that subdues elements of *talchum*, while emphasizing on-site realism by actually visiting sites of issue such as agricultural or industrial areas, as exemplified by *Hampyeong Sweet Potatoes*, *Solve the Case of Dong-Il Textiles*, and *Labor's Torch*; and plays adapted in *madanggeuk* style, generally staged on athletics grounds or outdoors by university theatrical coteries, such as *Vagabond Theater Troupe*, *A Dream of Pigs*, and *Slave Ownership Paper*.

A common feature among these plays is the call for criticism against military dictatorship, eradication of corruption, promotion of labor rights, and guarantee of democratic freedom.

Though each production differs considerably, *madanggeuk* is generally composed as follows. A *madanggeuk* consists of short episodes depicting simple tensions and conflicts, rather than an Aristotelian plot conveying a consistent and logical arrangement of incidents, alongside the sporadic inclusion of dancing scenes according to the compositional principle of *talchum*. For instance, conflicts such as those between farmers and the government regarding rice imports or between labors and entrepreneurs were presented through a number of short episodes, between which performers occasionally demonstrated a satirical dance with the unique traditional steps of *talchum*, thus generating keen empathy between the audience and the fictional characters languishing under oppression. Performers in *madanggeuk* often wear masks to convey archetypal characters based on social class or political conflicts. Temporal and spatial settings are managed without restriction and the performance is sometimes accompanied by a narrator, which is a facet generally found in *pansori*. The narratives generally end with a turn in a positive direction, indicating victory over oppressors. Just as ancient farmers played music to herald the commencement of agricultural rituals, *madanggeuk* begins as musicians and performers play traditional musical instruments such as *piri* (bamboo oboe), *buk* (small drum), and *janggu* (hourglass-shaped drum), and circle the performance venue to enliven the audience. The ending is finalized with the *dwitpuri* with cheerful music and dance participated by the play's characters, the audience, and other contributors to the performance. Sometimes light snacks and beverages are served during the wrap-up festivity.

The 1970s witnessed the formation of *madanggeuk*, and it was after 1980s that its concept was widely accepted and began to gain influence. As the escalation of military dictatorship coincided with heightened interest and support towards *madanggeuk*, similar forms of performance appeared and disappeared under slightly different names over the late 1970s and early 1980s. *Madanggeuk* movements flourished in earnest in the 1980s, however, followed by internal ideological conflicts and structural confusion.

It is interesting to find that although *madanggeuk* denounced Western theater and clamored for nationalism, it was not necessarily the case that the movement solely drew its roots from traditional performing arts or totally excluded influences from foreign theater. A major director in 1980s *madanggeuk*, Kim Seok-man recalled that, a year before the staging of his production *Jinogwi-gut*, he watched *A Tale of Two Cities*, an experimental play by Japan's Jokyo Gekijo Theater Company, written by Kara Juro, a Japanese experimental playwright and director. Kim was

Madanggeuk (Photo © Yonhap News)

greatly impressed by the dynamics created by actors and actresses running among and from the audience during the performance, which was staged on the outdoor tennis courts at Sogang University.[21] Indeed, the aspiration to unify the performers and the audience is a theme also found in the theatrical structure of the Drama Center and Oh Tae-suk's productions.

Modernization of tradition was not only a goal for anti-dictatorship movements led by university students or experiments by the Drama Center, but also for well-known playwrights and coterie theater companies including the Shilhum Theater Group and the Theatre Group Minye. Yun Dae-seong emerged in the theatrical arena as he attempted to combine Western dramaturgy with *talchum* to express strong discontent towards authority and social structure. His 1969 production, *Maknani*, criticizes the incompetent government and greedy bureaucrats during the Japanese invasion of Joseon in 1592 from the perspective of the general public. Settings for characters, such as the veteran or the servant, and the free transitions in time and space marked new attempts for the period. *Eat Up and Go Away* was a performance based on shamanic rituals and performed in 1972 at the Café Théâtre, intended to comically satirize the zeitgeist of mammonism and disregard for life through lascivious dialogue between the blind person and the *mudang*.[22] *Slave Ownership Paper* of 1973 was a dynamic and open dramatization of slaves' resistance in the Goryeo period (918-1392) featuring *talchum* characters, Nojang (debauched monk) and Chwibari (playboy). The Shilhum Theater Group also staged modernized versions of classical Korean novels in the form of traditional performing art, including *Chunhyangjeon* (The Story of Chunhyang) and

Heosaengjeon (*The Story of Heosaeng*) in 1970.

However, these productions remained limited as the conceptual products of playwrights and incomplete staging experiments. It was the Theatre Group Minye led by Heo Kyu that specifically and consistently took the lead in the succession and adoption of tradition in the 1970s. After establishing the Theatre Group Minye in 1973 under the objective of "creating original theatrical semiotics to develop dramatic arts unique to the Korean people," Heo Kyu heralded an ambitious beginning with *Seoul Malttugi*, written by Jang So-hyeon and directed by Sohn Jin-chaek, a production that criticizes the realities of the time through the *talchum* character Malttugi (servant). Afterwards, *Muldoridong* and *Dasiragi*, written and directed by Heo Kyu, swept many awards; the former is based on a legend surrounding the production process of *talchum* against the backdrop of a village called Muldori-dong; and the latter is a performance reimagining a shamanic ritual based in Jindo Island as the convergence of universal issues, such as death and life, this world and the next world, laughter and fear, tragedy and comedy. A point of difference from the Drama Center and university activism was that many performers in Minye were extremely skilled in traditional dance and songs as many had inherited *talchum* from past masters or studied *pansori* or folk songs. Unfortunately, however, the outstanding ability of Minye artists to recreate the unique aspects of traditional

Seoul Malttugi directed by Sohn Jin-chaek, 1973 (Photo © Yonhap News)

performing arts was not matched by philosophical and aesthetic considerations as to why and how such aspects could be adopted and modernized. Consequently, many Minye productions remained a simple combination of folk dance and song with traditional stories, out of context with the sensibilities of modern theater.

Most successful productions by Minye were plays of which dramaturgical structure and methods of expression were adopted from traditional theater, mask dramas in particular, with the addition of current issues and perspectives. Such works include *Nolbudyeon* (*The Story of Nolbu*), *Seoul Malttugi*, and *Dancing Malttugi*—all comedies that satirize corruption and irony of reality through the main *talchum* character Malttugi, which are evaluated as relatively successful cases of modern adoptions of traditional theater. Choi In-hoon's original *Nolbudyeon*,[23] dealing with a kind elder brother and a greedy younger brother in the Korean classical novel, was very successful in demonstrating the playwright's sharp awareness of retrospection from the present perspective and the attempt to develop a new Korean-style form by utilizing *pansori*'s unique introductory *chang* (traditional narrative song) and long lines of dialogue. Minye's other successful productions featured theatrical motifs and modes for expression entirely in keeping with traditional theater or performing arts, including *Baebaengi-gut* and *Dasiragi*. As for *Dasiragi*, it is meaningful to reflect on the lives and values of the Korean people from shamanic rituals on an island in Jeolla-do Province; but as for *Baebaengi-gut*, a question can be raised on whether to accept the work as a contemporary theatrical piece if it merely restored and reproduced the content and form as it was in the pre-modern age. Lastly, *Changpogaksi* (The Bride of Iris), *Muldoridong*, and *Jeongeupsa* (Song of Jeongeup) merely employ synopses or plot elements borrowed from classical literature, myths, and traditional performing arts, invoking the atmosphere of traditional theater with the typical dance movements, chang, or poetic lines, and nonetheless remain at the standard of melodrama or conventional romantic drama relying upon Western dramaturgy.

Non-realistic Playwrights

The period of 1970s featured the influence of Western experimental drama and recovery of tradition. It was also the period in the history of Korean drama which produced remarkable plays that surpassed realism. Renowned novelist Choi In-hoon strived to respond to the question of defining the identity of the Korean people, and while he sought the answer from traditional Korean stories, he finally found the answer not in the form of novels, but drama. He believed that traditional stories containing a people's primitive imagination and collective subconscious could be expressed better in the genre of drama due to the openness and availability of the performance in comparison to novels, which demands specific description. Choi published remarkable dramas in the 1970s. His staging techniques extended possibilities in terms of staging, time, and space to an almost limitless extent by robustly employing the genre traits of drama, for example, by reducing lines of dialogue; setting a character as a stutterer; and using long, beautiful passages closer to poetry, as opposed to short and sparsely deployed lines of dialogue.

Where Shall We Meet in What Form? (1970) depicts the cycle of the relationship and love between Princess Pyeonggang and Ondal the Fool that transcends life and death. *Once Upon a Long Time Ago* (1976) is a drama that describes the pain and salvation of the impoverished parents forced to strangle

Where Shall We Meet in What Form? directed by Kim Jeong-ok, 1970
(reproduced by Han Tae-sook, 2009) (Photo © Yonhap News)

their baby to death as the baby was born with wings and thus
branded as a rebel. The work links the universal concept of the
anti-messiah with a Korean folktale and maintains a balanced
structure in terms of the dramaturgy, while conveying
natural fear through the performance by using the stuttering
character to critical acclaim. *When Spring Comes to Hills and
Fields* (1977) presents the folktale of a leper driven away from
the community through the character afflicted with a stutter.
Choi concludes the ideas of tragedy and the limitations of
life innate in the basic psychology of the Korean people with
open utopian thought, unlike in Western drama. Despite
failing to completely embody the limitless poetic imagination
embedded in drama, most of his theatrical works succeeded
as representational performances prevalent in that time. In
particular, the most impressive of his achievements are two

different versions of the same play, *When Spring Comes to Hills and Fields*, directed by Yu Deok-hyeong as discussed earlier and by Sohn Jin-chaek; and these two productions effectively expressed the unique mythological traits embedded in Choi In-hoon's drama as a means of theatrical expansion. Up to the present day, his dramas continued to be challenged by ambitious directors and stage artists.

Amid the prevalent atmosphere of modernization of tradition in the 1970s, Lee Hyun-hwa and Lee Kang-baek published dramas based on Western modernism or original allegories. Unlike other Korean playwrights, Lee Hyun-hwa presented distinct plays bringing the gender issue to the forefront and escalating tension by creating an absurdist atmosphere, and his major works include *Sh-Sh-Shush*, depicting a couple forced to sexually submit to an unknown invader; *Who Is It?*, dealing with absurdist alienation and unfamiliarity between husband and wife; *Sanssitgim*, as discussed previously; *Cadenza*, in which a performer, initially sat among the audience as if a spectator, was brought to the stage to be seated on a chair and tortured to the point of submission; and *0.917*, the sensational story of a child sexually seducing an adult. Lee Gang-baek made his debut with *Five* (1971) and published *The Watchman* featuring political characteristics using rather ideological and allegorical dramaturgy; *Wedding*, which delves into the ultimate meaning of love between man and woman; and *The Jewel and the*

Woman depicting an artist's tenacity toward perfection.

Choi In-hoon and Lee Hyun-hwa were mainly active in the 1970s, while Lee Gang-baek actively published dramas until the 1990s, throughout which the main theatrical spaces included not only the Myeongdong National Theater and the Drama Center, but also smaller dedicated spaces developed by coterie theater companies launched in the 1960s, such as Shilhum Theater and Minye Theater, along with the establishment of the Samil-ro Changgo Theater and the Gonggan Theater, while the Café Théâtre, selling tea in the daytime and performing salon dramas at night, also served as a cultural attraction in Seoul. These small theaters were suitable for a variety of experimental plays in the 1970s with flexible stages and capacities of approximately 100 seats.

The 1970s was a period featuring the recovery of theatrical identity and enthusiasm for experimental styles; also a time of elite theater when both the practitioners and the audience encountered plays with an ideological, intellectual, and aesthetic approach. Many still view the 1970s as the artistic peak of Korean theater and rate no subsequent works as surpassing any performance of this period. On the other hand, productions of this time were criticized for their excessive preoccupation with formal experimentation to the point of neglecting the task of facing up to the definite and empirical reality.

03

Resurgence of Original Korean Theater and *Madanggeuk* in Anti-dictatorship Activism in the 1980s

South Korea of the 1980s appeared successful from the external perspective in terms of attaining material affluence and stability, while the same period saw the extreme aggravation of political and economic issues that had emerged since the Park Chung-hee administration, such as military dictatorship, obsessive dominance of anti-communism and national security in the political sphere, wealth imbalances, exploitation of labor, and diplomatic dependence on foreign powers. If Korean theater had enjoyed experimental and aesthetic theater based on traditional performing arts in the 1970s, it became engulfed in the anti-dictatorship movement against Chun Doo-hwan's Fifth Republic in the 1980s. By this point, *madanggeuk* had outstripped the aim of transmitting traditional performing arts and instead gained heightened attention in the social and cultural areas as a symbol of political resistance, exerting strong influence on theater performance overall. Among the non-mainstream theatrical circles performing *madanggeuk*, there was a prevailing viewpoint that any theatrical practitioners with a degree of intelligence and conscience must dedicate themselves to nationalist and populist ideology, while excluding modern Western aesthetics expressed in logical dramas and on proscenium stages. Much more attention and interest were given to indoor *madanggeuk* performed in small spaces, represented by the Theater Yeonwoo, than the 70s-style *madanggeuk* conventionally performed outdoors. Despite the prevailing cause of the era, it had failed to achieve maturity with regard to theatrical aesthetics in the 1980s. *Madanggeuk* was quite often involved in minor conflicts as it was closely monitored under the government's preemptive censorship policy. The policy of preemptive censorship was first introduced during the Japanese occupation for the authorities to thoroughly monitor all theatrical works prior to the performance, and was finally abolished in late 1998 as a result of democratization. After the late 1980s, political satires in small theaters diverged from the concept of *madanggeuk* to freely develop with a variety of experimental formats, which is a trend that persisted up to the 1990s.

In the 1950s to 1960s, translated productions imported from overseas prevailed, but the period of 1970s to 1980s saw Korean original theaters replace translations. The major factors behind this change in trend are as follows: increased interest in unfair social realities and the active expression of the desire to portray the lives of the general public across Korean theater in the 1980s; persistent attempts since the 1970s to transmit traditional Korean styles; continuation of institutional support to promote original plays through such means as the Korean Theater Festival, for example; and following the increased familiarity of Western drama through TV or video materials, the audiences' desire for the stage to present relatable stories as opposed to the amateurish imitation of westerners. Other factors include a decline in the number of high-level theater companies and the necessary human and material resources for high-quality performance of translated plays, and a possible financial burden to be imposed, if minimal, on theater companies as a result of the implementation of international copyright laws.

Although the quantity of original plays was higher than that of translated ones, the theatrical quality failed to surpass those performed in the 1970s, perhaps due to excessive nationalist influences that largely shunned drama-based Western plays. The theatrical establishment was once inundated with solo performances and novel adaptations featuring the arbitrary application of traditional performing arts, due to the influence of *madanggeuk* and populism. Among such plays were productions with strong social influence but rather unrefined quality in terms of theatrical aesthetics. Meanwhile, in the government-led Korean Theater Festival, major playwrights such as Yun Jo-byeong, Lee Kang-baek, and Yun Dae-seong presented dramatic works that transcended realism, continuing to produce literature-based works.

If it can be said that the 1980s featured strong messages and weak interest in aesthetics, Oh Tae-suk and Kim Jeong-ok presented productions with high levels of artistic completion and utilization of traditional performing arts. The former ironically unraveled the bitter grief caused by scars left from the war and collapse of Korean values, as a form of dramatic entertainment combined with his unique sense of Korean tradition, while the latter collaborated with stage artist Lee Byung-boc in producing Korean-style farces imbued with not only the Korean sense of traditional beauty, but also mise-en-scène, costume, and props, to a level of contemporary refinement sufficient to impress Western artists, and took the lead in presenting his works to the world. The most notable director in the 1980s is arguably Ki Kook-seo; having established a theater company in 1976, Ki passed the 1980s without being influenced by any particular source and presenting post-modernist works as if in anticipation of the 1990s. His *Hamlet* series, a radical deconstruction and reinterpretation of the original Shakespearean play, through which he acutely and sensuously described thematic issues, such as military dictatorship, the violent pursuit of pleasure in the urban culture, and the destruction of humanity.

Madanggeuk Going Indoors

During the formative period of the 1970s, *madanggeuk* drew extraordinary attention from the societal and cultural domains for the combination of traditional performing arts and a finely tuned sense of critical thought. As the 1980s emerged, however, *madanggeuk* remained at a standstill with no concrete progress in terms of theatrical aesthetics. *Madanggeuk* of this time placed the first and foremost priority on the sincere unity between the audience as the general public (*minjung* in Korean) and the practitioners. The performance generally started with the *apnori*, followed by a number of episodes accompanying various dances and songs, and ended with a wrap-up festivity, *dwitpuri*. Thus the performances gradually became devoid of liveliness and sentimental depth in terms of the actual theatrical expression.

Following the rapid political changes of the early 1980s, *madanggeuk* attempted to advance to the next level, along with a variety of cultural performances with progressive inclinations. As opposed to the superficial adoption of traditional performing arts, such as *talchum, madanggeuk* generally assumed either the characteristics of *madang-gut*, connoting open-space shamanistic rituals and focusing on situational sincerity, collective enthusiasm, scenic movements, and populist typicality, or otherwise the features of *minjokgeuk* (national identity theater), which reinforced the aspect of political ideology; in other words, the theatrical art of overcoming the national reality of a divided Korea to identify a sense of national reality from the perspective of the people. Despite these attempts, these two forms of theater failed to break the standstill and instead faced criticism for narcissistic ideality and vague tautology. Exhausted with ideological disputes, *madanggeuk* attempted to combine itself with conventional theater plays in the 1980s as a way to induce a breakthrough. For example, *A Hawk of Jangsangot* and *A Story of Mr. Rabbit* were considered the first attempts to this aim: The former was a performance that introduced collective mask dance of the outdoor *madanggeuk* into the indoor stage of the Drama Center; and the latter was the introduction of the open spatial concept and relaxed progression in *mandanggeuk* to the stage of the Drama Center. Afterwards, *madanggeuk* gradually changed in nature and began to be adapted to smaller stages, such as Mirinae Theater and Yeonwoo Theater.

Consequently, "indoor *madanggeuk*" was mainly based around fledgling theater companies, such as Yeonwoo and Arirang, and dedicated to configuring the amalgamation of *madanggeuk* and conventional theater aesthetics within the confines of a small stage shaped like a black box, thereby succeeding in attracting a young and intellectually conscious audience. Indoor *madanggeuk* can be categorized as three types for the sake of discussion. First is the straightforward indoor adaptation of outdoor *madanggeuk*, consisting of a performance area surrounded by the audience, often featuring dances and musical performances, and adhering to the original structure of *talchum* or outdoor *madanggeuk* characterized as "*apnori* + short episodes + *dwitpuri*." This category includes works such as *Jamneopuri* and *Mincho*, productions in the early period of indoor *madanggeuk*. The second type maintains this basic structure with the addition of the spectacles and effects available in indoor stages, such as arrangement of the audience, motion lines, lighting, group dances, and ensembles. This category includes *A Hawk of Jangsangot*; *A Story of Mr. Rabbit*; *Who Owns that Stopped Coffine?*; *Pannori Arirang Hill*; and *Gabose Gabose* (Shall We Go, Shall We Go). The third category connotes productions based on dialogue between a small number of performers, generally short, simple, and spontaneous plays including *Slugs*; *Dreams of the Strong*; *Arirang*; *Numbness*; and *The Hometown, Where I Used to Live*. Despite demonstrating seriousness in their staging intention, passion on the stage, and authenticity of the performance including the dances, said productions received negative reviews from prominent figures in theatrical circles for the crudeness of consciousness not sublimated into art and de-aestheticization.[24] However, certain productions were more successful in receiving positive reviews from the audience and theater critics, and the case in point was *A Chronicle of Mr. Han*. This production accepted the basic characteristics of outdoor *madanggeuk* such as the critical attitude, epic

A Chronicle of Mr. Han directed by Kim Seok-man, 1985 (Photo © Yonhap News)

narrative structure, focus on enjoyment, and audience participation, while emphasizing literary features focusing on dialogue, individual realism and liveliness in the description of characters, and delicate sensibilities of indoor space in terms of staging and performance.

A Chronicle of Mr. Han (directed by Kim Seok-man, 1985), a production based on the novel of the same title by Hwang Sok-yong, is a story that exposes the tragedy of the divided Korea through the destructive progress of Han Yeong-deok, an obstetrician and gynecologist who defects to South Korea from North Korea. His story is interspersed with political incidents such as the Yalta Conference (1945), the circumstances surrounding the division of the Korean Peninsula along the 38th parallel, the outbreak of the Korean War (1950-1953), and corruption within the Rhee Syngman administration, through mediums such as verbal narration, a play within a play, dance, and mime. Just as theatrical director Kim Seok-man specified his intention to move beyond the tragedy of an individual's life and instead embody the greater significance that defined the said life, in relation to ideology and the dynamics of international politics, the production places the majority of its focus on the historical context or historical perspectives of national division. However, the decision to formally simplify and reflect life in keeping with the conventions of *madanggeuk* and its subsequent expression through simple and effective means of communication such as songs and dance resulted in the negligence of the complexity and specificity inherent in the dynamic between individuals and the world. For instance, in a scene explaining the nation's division along the 38th parallel, General George Marshall of the U.S. Army and his subordinates perform an exaggerated dance to carelessly stomp on a map of Korea spread on the ground like carpet, and in another scene, the investigators interrogating Han Yeong-deok are caricatured and stereotyped to an extreme to emphasize the travesty through acting, which may have been effective in delivering the political context, but appeared somewhat in congruous with other scenes expressing the agonizing thoughts of the main character.

In the late 1980s, Theater Yeonwoo endeavored to find a breakthrough with free-form social satire without strict adherence to the form of *madanggeuk*. These attempts included *Chil-soo and Man-soo* directed in 1986 by Lee Sang-woo, wittily depicting two isolated young men who paint billboards on high-rise buildings; *Even Birds Leave the World* directed by Kim Seok-man, employing collaborative creation using various images to embody the poetry of Hwang Ji-woo, which illustrate his despair towards the times; and *A Story of Old Thieves* written and directed by Lee Sang-woo in 1989, a farce of two thieves who break into the mansion of a high official, fiercely satirizing corruption in positions of power gained attention and positive review from the audience and critics alike. Independent from Theater Yeonwoo since 1996, Lee Sang-woo founded a theater company Trans-Dimensional Stageship and has since produced original political comedies such as *Bi Eon So*, meaning "toilet," compiling episodes of public toilets for an ironic portrayal of the false consciousness of intellectuals; and *Boar Hunting* that satirizes mankind's limitless greed by depicting the commotion caused by a boar through the simple repetition of dramatic rhythms. After the collapse of communism, however, this kind of political satire theater lost its main target of criticism and presaged the emergence of desperation and nihilism rife in the 1990s.

Madanggeuk in the 1980s was launched amid high social and cultural expectations, but was overwhelmed by the ideological disputes of the era, without the theoretical and aesthetic study required to translate such aspects into performance, subsequently falling into decline with

Chil-soo and Man-soo directed by Lee Sang-woo, 1986
(reproduced in 2007 by Theater Yeonwoo) (Photo © Yonhap News)

the collapse of left-wing ideologies in the late 1980s. Retrospectively, the significance of *madanggeuk* can be evaluated as presenting a theatrical form sharing common aspects with popular theater in the Third World including the Philippines and South America; political theater dealing with socio-political issues; the successor to traditional theatrical aesthetics; and aspects of post-modernism.[25] *Madanggeuk* is also congruent with the post-modernist theater prevalent in the 1990s due to its non-representational character, greater appeal to the senses than in terms of language, and desire to actively communicate with the audience. Furthermore, if a case can be cited for having continued the process of theatrical

Madang nori by Michoo Theatre Company (Photo © Yonhap News)

embodiment through to the 1990s and achieving a degree of success, it is likely to be that of *madang nori*, a form of *madanggeuk* developed by Michoo Theatre Company for the commercialization and expansion of the art form. *Madang nori* as a performance received popular affection for gathering into a stadium an audience consisting of thousands of people who had been unfamiliar with the theatrical art form, to share in the experience of an open space, light satirical comedy, archetypal characters and episodic structures, theatrical spectacles, and communication among the audience.

The Korean Theater Festival

Launched in 1977 with the aim to promote original plays, the Korean Theater Festival continued to produce original theaters in the 1980s. It is no exaggeration to say that the Korean Theater Festival served to present most major plays by professional theater companies in the 1980s. This period was notable for the fervent public interest and influence given to the progressive theatrical ideology and aesthetics of fringe theater such as *madanggeuk* or *minjokgeuk*, and therefore, it was not surprising that the status of the Korean Theater Festival had diminished in relative terms. Yet theatrical pieces presented for the festival could not be free from the social burden imposed by the period either, and many of such works conveyed a strong sense of social and historical consciousness in a heavy and didactical atmosphere without neglecting issues of social distress. This type of theater, therefore, did not deviate from the conventional aesthetic trend of Western-style modern theater, instead generally revolving around the scope of revised or eclectic realism to produce works with a variety of modes and values.

These features are well reflected in the following playwrights. A rarity among playwrights of the 1980s, Yun Jo-byeong was steadfast in his adherence to orthodox realism and depicted the lives of isolated human beings set in farming and fishing areas or coal mines. Yun was a prolific playwright, having published a play nearly every year to form a broad bibliography including *Farmland, A Peasant Woman, Peasants, The Sound of the Reed Organ, Morning Dew on the Bonfire,* and *From the Crescent till the Dark Moon.* The former three depict the hardy lives of rural people as they resolve to defend their land in the face of changes brought about by modernization. The rest of Yun's works attempt to portray different aspects of hardships in life: *Morning Dew on the Bonfire* relays the brutal screams of miners trapped in a collapsed mine as they clamor to live; *The Sound of the Reed Organ,* the dignified lives of women who overcame obstacles of modern history, including sexual slavery under Japanese occupation; and *From the Crescent till the Dark Moon,* the dreams and despairs of life conveyed through characters in mines and fishing villages. His works are characterized by the vivid description of isolated lives from economic, social, and historical perspectives, and the unfailing proclivity to capture the ontological question as to the true nature of human life.

Along with Yun Jo-byeong, Lee Kang-baek was also actively engaged in writing activities in the 1980s, making yearly appearances at theatrical festivals. Lee is known for his presentation of sharp social awareness and strict moral concerns through his plays, including *Family Genealogy,* addressing moral corruption and the sense of guilt; *The Jurassic People,* which depicts the contrasting positions and conflicts of conscience among twelve people who find themselves

Chilsanri directed by Jeong Jin-soo, 1989 (Photo © Yonhap News)

involved in the explosion of a mine in a coal-mining town; *Homo Separatus*, portraying the pain of a divided country through the love between a man and a woman; *Spring Day*, contemplating the issues of life and death, elderliness and youth, possession and deprivation sublimated into poetic imagery; *Biong Saong*, a reproduction of *Onggojipjeon* (The Story of an Obstinate Old Man) from the contemporary perspective; *Falling Asleep After Eating Utopia*, depicting the anguish of an intellectual caught between the ideologies of conservatives and radical progressives; and *Chilsanri* (meaning "a village surrounded by seven mountain peaks"), illustrating the motherhood of women whose children have become communist partisans in post-war Korea. Lee Kang-baek's morality and logic often manifest in allegorical situations and character settings, leading to the evaluation that Lee's productions are "exquisite and intricate like a Persian carpet."[26] On the other hand, his works are limited by factors, such as ideality devoid of actualized characters and behavior, artificial situations, and closed plot structures.

Jeong Bok-geun, the only female playwright notable for active theatrical contributions in the 1980s, demonstrated a solid sense of history to ruminate upon the spirit of the Korean people through plays, such as *Black Bird* depicting General Lee Jing-ok of Joseon as a revolutionary nationalist, and *The Keeper* dealing with the preservation of the national spirit and struggle for survival through a family of peddlers in the enlightenment period. Jeong also released some controversial works, such as *Silent Scream* and *The Poisoned Chalice* that describe the self-esteem and scar of a woman living in a period of political turbulence; and *House Caught in a Trap* that presents the female perspective on family breakdown caused by sexual violence. The work of Jeong Bok-geun was critically noted for asserting a strong sense of morality and thematic consciousness while simultaneously employing dialogue with psychological depth and refinement.

Other writers with empirical interests in socio-political issues include Lee Jae-hyun, who wrote *Red and White* to publicize the issue of prisoners of war, in which he had long held an interest; *We Live in the United States*, a description of lives of immigrants in the U.S.; and *Koreagate*, which dramatizes the incident of Korean-American lobbyist Kim Han-jo. On the other hand, Yun Dae-seong veered away from his initial interest in traditional performing arts and published *Mythology 1900*, a psycho drama based on a true police investigation, and *Breaking the Wall* that deals with the dissolution of the colonial legacy. Other productions include Roh Gyeong-sik's *Odolttogi*, describing the confrontation between Catholicism and folk religions through the 1901 uprising led by Lee Jae-su in Jejudo Island, and *The Country as Far Away as the Sky*, a story of families separated by the division of the Korean Peninsula; Kim Eui-kyung's *An Anarchist from the Colony* that illuminates the life of anarchist Park Yeol, and *Searching for the Lost History* addressing the massacre of Koreans in the Great Kanto earthquake in 1923.

An Anarchist from the Colony directed by Jeong Jin-soo, 1984 (Photo © Yonhap News)

As such, 1980s productions released at the Korean Theater Festival dealt with strong motifs of social and historical awareness, and were pointed out to be generally heavy in tone and designed to offer moral lessons. In terms of form, the abovementioned plays shared traits in common with other political plays of the decade including *madanggeuk*, in the fact that they maintained realistic representation and contained strong narrative elements. From the dramaturgical perspective, the plays generally featured narrative elements deviating from those of conventional realism, including a commentator, narration, monologues, frequent transition in space and time, a play within a play, and retrospection.

Launch of Mokwha Repertory Company by Oh Tae-suk

Aside from such prevalent trends of the time, a number of original plays contributed to the prosperity of the theatrical arts during the 1980s, exemplified by the unique creative worlds presented by Oh Tae-suk and Kim Jeong-ok, whose activities began in the 1960s or 1970s and developed through the subsequent decades to establish distinct theatrical realms in which tradition, modern sensibilities, and indirect commentary on reality merge and intertwine. Their productions presented a strong experimental sense and intense interest in Korean tradition as the continuation of customary trends during the 1970s, along with the ideal co-existence with modernity, which presaged the emergence of the post-modernist tendency of the 1990s.

Starting with one-act plays of modernist inclinations, Oh Tae-suk created a buzz in the 1970s as a playwright and director of various productions, such as *Chobun, Tae, Soettugi Nori, A Medicine Seller,* and *Chunpung's Wife,* continuing to attract public attention to the greater diversity of themes and stage language entering the 1980s. Although Oh's work during the 1980s featured a wide range of aspects, the underlying core theme was the simultaneous pursuit of his constant interest in tradition and folklore, alongside the pain and suffering caused by the Korean War and modernization, in the attempt to capture the image of the Korean people that he had sought after through reflection upon not only the past, but the lives of the present in modern and contemporary Korea. For instance, *May in 1980* duplicates the image of cafés at the eponymous period in hyper-realistic detail; *Hanmanseon* (*The Train between Korea and Manchuria*) juxtaposes the ordinary daily life of a crane rental agent with the heroic life of Korean patriot Ahn Jung-geun; *Africa,* an inaugural performance of the Mokwha Repertory Company, tells of the joys and sorrows of overseas laborers in connection with social incidents at home and abroad; and *Vinyl House* exposes the dehumanization of modern bureaucratic society. Other productions include *Cornus Fruit* and *A Bicycle,* influenced by

Hanmanseon directed by Oh Tae-suk, 1981
(Photo © National Theater of Korea)

the author's experience of the war and death that dominates his unconsciousness; *Intimacy between Father and Son* that uses the concepts of death and sexuality to depict the extremes in human relationships; *Song of Women* and *Mother* that explore the idealistic image of a Korean woman; and *Dream of an Ordinary Man*, dealing with the Korean ideals of humanity within traditional literature and mythology through the use of meta-logical imagination and humor.

In particular, *Intimacy between Father and Son, Vinyl House,* and *A Bicycle* are highlighted as the representative masterpieces among Oh's works in the 1980s: *Intimacy between Father and Son*, a demonstration of Oh's ruthless instincts as a director featuring the black comedy depiction of

Intimacy between Father and Son directed by Oh Tae-suk, 1987
(Photo © Mokwha Repertory Company)

Vinyl House directed by Oh Tae-suk, 1989
(Photo © Yonhap News)

a father-son relationship between the historical figures King Yeongjo (r. 1724-1776) and his son Crown Prince Sado, which becomes distorted due to extreme greed; *Vinyl House* that uses the allegory of a greenhouse to criticize the state of Korean society; and *A Bicycle* dealing with the lingering scar left by the Korean War, restructured through the collective guilt and unconsciousness of rural villagers. In *A Bicycle*, the collective guilt among the villagers from the experience of having been both the perpetrators and victims of the mass massacre during the Korean War, unfurls in a reconstituted form through the recollection of the village scribe after he returns from a state of unconsciousness lasting 40 days that began upon experiencing unknown hallucinations. The subsequent process of traversing backwards in time unleashes episodes depicting the memories, guilt and fear of each villager through reality, dreams, illusions, the scribe's narration, and flashbacks in a hectic manipulation of time and space. At the core of the collective guilt stand the community center in which community leaders were confined and burned, and the unknown perpetrator who set fire to the center.

Since the establishment of the Mokwha Repertory Company in 1984, Oh Tae-suk presented independent and original stages with his theatrical ensemble. The imaginative power in Oh's dramatic direction is unleashed as early as the initial planning step, resulting in the liberal enmeshment, condensation and rapid progression of time and space within the theatrical composition, which is then punctuated just as freely by visual elements such as unexpected objects from ordinary life, exaggerated forms of dolls or costumes. His productions are sometimes criticized for ambiguity in the absence of even the slightest sense of objectivity, arbitrary development, and abuse of fragmentary visual ideas. All these elements, however, are fused and liberated to create events of sheer exhilaration and entertainment, combined with the writer's characteristic folksy language and traditional Korean rhythms. Going through the 1980s, his theater became evaluated positive for its "inspired performance, enthusiasm, liveliness, and vitality,"[27] while "best revealing the true character and identity of Koreans."[28]

However, Oh's characteristically Korean style of imagination was not completely free from the influence of overseas experimental theater. It is said that after seeing experimental Western plays by Tadeusz Kantor and Michael Kirby in New York in 1979, he realized and was convinced that experimental theater in the West bears a striking similarity with Korean tradition. Furthermore, entering the 1980s, he learned of Japanese contemporary theater including dramas written by Kara Juro. Oh Tae-suk established himself as a leading theatrical figure through 1980s and after his 1990 play, *Why Did Sim Cheong Plunge into the Indang Sea Twice?*, his moral fury and messages to society became much more potent over the 1990s.

Jayu Theater Company: Display of Traditional Korean Beauty toward the World

Having specialized in French drama since the 1960s, Kim Jeong-ok began to explore Korean-style drama, such as *Evening Primrose, Flowers Bloom Even on Windy Days, A Blood Wedding, Hen Instead of Cock, then Even the Hen, Then They Lay Dying*, after directing *What Will Become of Us?* in 1978. He was keenly aware of international trends in theater due to frequent encounters with the outside world through activities in the International Theatre Institute (ITI), and succeeded in conveying uniquely Korean sentiments in an eloquent form of theatrical language which was universal and refined on a global scale. Kim's deep interest in the Korean conception of death was expressed through the amalgamation of various styles such as total theater, epic theater, liturgical drama, and general entertainment, with the aim of conveying the uniquely Korean sentiment that traverses between life and death, specifically focusing on death among the masses as represented by the clown, the concept of *han* as the deep sorrow and resentment permeating such deaths, and ultimately the resolution thereof. His plays were intended to serve as both memorial rites and entertainment in tribute to the nameless deaths of the people-clowns and to symbolize liberation from all constraints in terms of Eastern or Western notions of theatrical form. He described his theater as a "performer-centered play" or a "collectivist creative dramas" as well as the new concept of the "third play," in which legacies of traditional Korean performing arts and Western dramas collide creatively.

One of Kim Jeong-ok's most prominent plays is the Jayu Theater Company's *What Will Become of Us?*, which was re-staged on several occasions throughout the 1980s after its premiere in 1970. The story, adapted from the folktale of a man and a woman who transform into *jangseung*,[29] or village guardian posts, upon dying under wrongful circumstances and failing to requite their shared love, is deconstructed into a tragicomedy using elements, such as remarks, commentary, dance and song, entertainment, and rituals as exercises in extemporaneousness and collective creativity, embodied by clowns as allegories for the people. As the story progresses, the intervals between scenes are punctuated with each character entering the stage to perform *chang, pansori*, dance, jokes, or musical performance, exposing themselves freely and easily as performers. Kim viewed the performers as the main symbols of his theatrical world and expected spontaneous displays of collective creativity; yet his attempts did not always end successfully. Lee Byung-boc's costumes and objects abundant in Korean characteristics and refined sensibilities greatly contributed to Kim Jeong-ok's work in directing the form of total theater with the aim to express sentiments unique to Korean culture, and received much praise from Europeans. Kim's productions were highly reputed at home and abroad for featuring "the free combination of tragedy and comedy, sophistication and vulgarity, poetry and the epic,"[30] and "the appealing lightness in acceptance of both life and death."[31] However, his works were also criticized for "lacking the structural power and strong imagery to tie together all constituent elements,"[32] in spite of the repeated use of similar themes and forms, and revealing the somewhat sentimental message.

Michoo Theatre Company: Modernization of Traditional Performing Arts

Another factor worthy of mention is in relation to Sohn Jin-chaek's productions in the Michoo Theatre Company, which Sohn established in 1986 after he left the Theatre Group Minye, through which he had been active in the 1970s. Following the inaugural performances of *The Keeper* in 1986 and *The Toenails of General Oh* in the following year, Sohn began to pursue productions that continued to safeguard traditions as he had with the Minye in the 1970s, while reflecting contemporary characteristics. The inaugural play *The Keeper*, written by Jeong Bok-geun and directed by Sohn, is a highly modern production that traces back to ancient history and deals with the strong spirit of the Korean people, while exploring dramatic expressions and employing dramatic characters in various ways that freely cross through time and space. The narrative of the performance featured a circular structure starting with a funerary ritual in the Kim clan, a family of considerable wealth in Kaesong, North Korea, and ending with another ancestral rite. The narration of the old man as the commentator and the transitional uses of lighting and slides illustrate a mosaic-like reconstruction that reverses the current of time from present events to ancient history.

The Michoo Theatre Company's second regular performance was *The Toenails of General Oh*, written by Park

The Keeper directed by Sohn Jin-chaek, 1986 (Photo © Michoo Theatre Company)

Jo-yeol and directed by Sohn Jin-chaek. Although the play was actually written in 1974, it was not staged until years later as the underlying socio-political messages resulted in its inclusion on the list of prohibited performances administered by the public performance ethics committee under the military regime. The allegory of an innocent young man from the countryside being victimized by the bureaucratic military system and dominant political ideology unfolded in three parts: the scenes embodying the bucolic atmosphere of the country complete with an anthropomorphized cow, the protagonist's mother, and his wife named Kkotbuni, portrayed using masks and formal movements; followed by the caricatured scenes of mechanical rigidity of the militarized society; and grim scenes displaying the young man's tragic death. These two performances were first milestones for the Michoo Theatre Company that signaled a departure from the Minye-style modernization of tradition and emphasized contemporary tendencies, thereby demonstrating enough promise to generate positive expectations for its future activities into the 1990s.

The Toenails of General Oh directed by Sohn Jin-chaek, 1987 (reproduced in 1997)
(Photo © Michoo Theatre Company)

Ki Kook-seo's *Hamlet* Series

Gathering cultured youths in their 20s to found the Theater Company 76 in 1976, Ki Kook-seo generally staged experimental dramas including Peter Handke's *Publikumsbeschimpfung* (*Offending the Audience*) and began to garner a reputation in the theatrical world. Although he lived through the 1980s, his productions were quite different from *madanggeuk* performances as vehicles of direct political propaganda or Oh Tae-suk and Kim Jeong-ok's auteurism-based productions. Ki's productions were also not greatly influenced by overseas dramas. Instead, Ki Kook-seo's *Hamlet* series constitute a vivid representation of a young theatrical practitioner in torturous suffering in the face of the political realities of the 1980s. Shocked by a series of political incidents from 1979 through 1981, such as the assassination of Park Chung-hee, the coup d'état by Chun Doo-hwan, and the subsequent Gwangju Democratic Movement, Ki was inspired to cast new insight into *Hamlet*. The *Hamlet* series (Parts I-V) boldly deconstructed the performances of the original, and went on to be staged from 1981 to the 1990s, thus occupying a fascinating position in the contemporary history of experimental theater in Korea.

Among his five *Hamlet* productions, the earlier three were performed in the 1980s. *Hamlet I*, staged in 1981, eliminates the acts and chapters in the original play to restructure the progression into 18 chapters, while making no big changes to the storyline and adjusting the final duel scene, whereby the duel is repeated three times: The first is the same as the one in the original play; the second results in Hamlet's death by Laertes's sword, upon which Horatio plots a rebellion, butchering the king and Laertes with his sword, in potent allegory of the repetition of history as Horatio's revolt comes soon after that of Claudius; the third also shows Horatio attempt a revolt, with a group and wielding guns in this case, which is directly satirical of the military regime led by Chun Doo-hwan. In the epilogue, there are rows of corpses to represent the May 18 Gwangju Massacre, followed by a brief scene in which a young man passes in front of the corpses with the emotional passivity of an unrelated spectator.

Staged in 1982, *Hamlet II: History of Terror and Insanity* defines certain political incidents as acts of terrorism and depicts the consequence of the resulting insanity that pervades the lives of individuals and society as a whole. Director Ki reinterprets characters as contemporary figures and in particular, set Rosencrantz and Guildenstern as violent homosexuals and constant drug abusers, respectively; Gertrude and Ophelia, as decadent women in the upper class; and Hamlet, as a weak character suffering from internal pain among other characters.

Unlike the previous productions, *Hamlet III*, staged in 1984, portrays the positive determination to overcome frustration and pain. The playwright deems the character of Hamlet as being too weak to build the sturdy determination to overcome hardships by himself, and therefore juxtaposes him with Orestes of Sartre's *Les Mouches* (*The Flies*), who faces circumstances not dissimilar to Hamlet's. Furthermore, borrowing his strong ontological resolution for resistance, Ki intended to "combine these two politically motivated works to show the despair of a weak intellect through *Hamlet*, and victory over suffering through the purity of mind in *The Flies*."[33] The performance was filled with effects to directly reference the political situation of the time, including roars of the protesting crowds, gunfire, electrical torture, and airborne troops, all hinting at the Gwangju resistance, and Hamlet agonizes over the question of whether "to participate or to spectate" with a toy gun in his hand instead of the customary skull. The dual performance lasted for five hours with *Hamlet* staged inside the theater in the Culture and Arts Center and *The Flies* performed in the theater lobby.[34] Though coarse as artistic productions, his plays were a direct response to the contemporary political situation, as well as a projection of post-modernist works prevalent in the 1990s Korean theater.

Introduction of Foreign Theater Productions and Diversification of Korean Plays

Arguably the first international theater festival in Korea, the Third World Theater Festival was held in 1981, demonstrating that even the military regime engaged with the theatrical world to a degree. However, its impact was minimal. It was not until the Seoul Olympic World Theater Festival of 1988 that foreign theater productions were properly introduced to Korea. Visiting performances included those by the Comédie-Française and the National Theater of Greece, alongside Brazilian and Czech theater and Japanese *kabuki*, and it was around this time that contemporary Japanese drama began to be introduced to Korea.

Not only due to Japan's 36-year colonial rule of Korea but also due to the similarities in Japan's cultural background and modern theatrical history, the introduction of contemporary Japanese drama exerted an influence on Korea, in a different sense from the introduction of contemporary Western drama. Among the productions introduced, *The Boiling Sea*, directed by Tsuka Kohei, and *The Water Station*, written and directed by Ota Shogo, aroused public interest in particular: The former features absurdly comic exaggeration performed by Korean actors and actresses, including Jeon Moo-song and Kim Ji Sook, respectively, to portray the investigation into the Atami Beach murder case; and the latter opened new possibilities in physical performance through the extremely deliberate movements of the performers' body and their accumulated energy. These two performances conveyed expressions of uniquely Japanese sentiments in a refreshing combination with the element of absurdist modernism. Furthermore, the play successfully exuded the discontinuity and inexplicability inherent in the atmosphere of post-modernism, generating shockwaves and an enormous impact on the craving for new expressions in Korean theater after the decline of *madanggeuk*.

As economic growth accelerated despite the military dictatorship due to strong industrial exports and construction booms in the Middle East, the 1980s was a burgeoning period of theatrical commercialization. Although a range of political problems continued to persist, Korea saw the continuous expansion of the theatrical world and the emergence of various forms of theater, along with steady economic growth. For instance, the productions of the Shilhum Theater Group including *Equus*, *Agnes of God*, and *Ireland* were met with great success, attracting larger audiences and subsequently expanding the underlying audience base; while the enhanced desire for entertainment among the public led to musicals being popularized on the theatrical scene.

Consequently, Daehangno was formed as a theater district occupied by the Culture and Arts Center and small-scale theaters, while outside Daehangno, larger theaters such as the Seoul Arts Center were established. The audience, previously dominated by university students, garnered greater demographical diversity. Various other theatrical endeavors included the Sanwoollim Theater's attempt to consolidate feminist theater to target middle-aged women, and director Kim U-ok, who opened the Dongrang Youth Theater Company and experimented with theater for children and youths, which received an enthusiastic response. As South Korea became a signatory to the Universal Copyright Convention in 1987 and began to pay royalties for foreign dramas written later than October 1, 1987, which led to the concern amid theatrical circles in Korea regarding the potential future consequence of heightened barriers towards staging Western dramas in Korea.

04

Postmodernist Spectacle and the Emergence of Young Directors in the 1990s

The end of the military dictatorship and the emergence of the civilian government under the Kim Young-sam administration, aided by external factors such as the collapse of communism across the Soviet Union and Eastern Europe in 1991, appeared to herald a rapid conclusion to the preponderance of politics and ideology in Korea. With the breakdown of ideology, Korean theater of the 1990s was embroiled into the waves of fin-de-siècle postmodernism. The previous targets of political attack and satire of the 1980s had become nonexistent, to be swept away by the global waves of postmodernism that rolled in and filled the void. In the absence of the suppressive influence of ideological theater characterized at the time by *madanggeuk*, those in the theatrical circles celebrated the sense of liberation in sensual images and deconstructive wit, body and object, and the sensibilities of popular culture. It was against this backdrop that new directors in their 30s and 40s appeared, including Lee Youn-taek, Chae Seung-hun, Choi Yong-hun, Kim Ara, Cho Kwang-hwa, who outwardly indulged in sensuality and amusement, whilst maintaining interests in issues such as power, history, and loss of humanity in a society of excessive consumerism.

With the sudden proliferation of theater companies and drama theaters of various sizes in the theater district of Daehangno, postmodernism became evident not only in the spectacles of large-scale theaters but also in the limited space of minor theaters. As Daehangno underwent a period of deterioration in the mid-1990s due to the rising rent prices and the spread of decadent entertainment, theatrical practitioners followed the Western example of off-off Broadway in establishing small-scale theaters around the cheaper area of Hyehwa-dong, opting to run the theaters collaboratively among several theatrical practitioners, a foremost example of which is Theater Company Hyehwa-dong 1st Number. Named after its address, the theater is equipped with only around 150 seats and a small adjustable stage, serving as an incubator for the vast majority of key playwrights and directors in the 1990s, and retains a certain degree of influence. Despite the confined space in intimate proximity with the audience, such theater artists attempted to surpass the original text of the drama or deconstruct the drama with the use of powerfully energetic stage imagery, bodies of actors, and a broad range of objects.

Established writer-directors such as Oh Tae-suk and Ki Kook-seo continued to show remarkably active contributions. Whether it was because new, original plays of decent quality had been rare or because the status of playwrights had diminished relative to that of directors and their alluring use of postmodernist senses, the 1990s marked the prevalence of deconstructed Western classics such as Shakespearean drama, which were directed in reconstructed form by many leading directors including Lee Youn-taek, Chae Seung-hun, Kim Ara, Cho Kwang-hwa, and Ki Kook-seo to the extent that, more than ten versions of *Hamlet* were staged repeatedly in a single year. A central keyword of deconstructionist methodology was tradition. As *madanggeuk* suffered from diminished popularity since the early 1990s, however, overall interest in the legacy of traditional theater saw a noticeable decline. A little of the interest remained only in the productions by Oh Tae-suk and Sohn Jin-chaek. Oh continued theatrical games combining traditional performing arts and social criticism. The politically critical *madanggeuk* of the 1980s had developed into *madang nori*, a form of large-scale traditional outdoor performance, which were pronounced in their postmodernist and commercial nature, and often held in a sizeable venue such as a gymnasium and designed for popular appeal to the masses. Furthermore, the greater freedom with which Koreans were able to travel abroad allowed for a greater volume of exchanges with theatrical circles in Asia and the West. From 1997, the International Theater Festival was held as an affiliated festival of the government-supported Seoul Theater Festival, inspiring the work of young directors in Korea by introducing both classical and modern plays from the U.S.,

France, Italy, Greece, Eastern Europe, and Japan, as well as theater companies of ethnic Koreans in Japan.

Lee Youn-taek: A Powerless Intellectual and a Showman on the Stage

In the 1990s, the most active contributor to theatrical circles in Seoul was arguably Lee Youn-taek, a playwright and director who led creative efforts with the Street Theatre Troupe (aka Theatre Troupe Georipae) in Busan. Lee's ardent creative urge and enthusiasm were applied to the contemplation of power, contemporary issues facing intellectuals of a tumultuous era, and the future prospect for the lives of the people. In terms of style, Lee's approach can be summarized as selective eclecticism, prone to employing a wide spectrum of styles from modernism and postmodernism, and presenting characteristics of traditional Korean drama mixed with elements from William Shakespeare, Georg Büchner, Tadeusz Kantor, and Heiner Müller. Aside from his talents as a poet, Lee was known as a showman with a deep understanding of the stage and his gift of rousing the audience.

Lee entered into the Seoul theatrical circles in 1989 with *Citizen K*, which he wrote and directed. This play is a compelling expressionist depiction of a journalist's feeling of powerlessness as an intellectual who was suppressed and tortured under the gloomy yoke of political oppression in the 1980s. The play uses intense and abstract language to convey destructive energy of the kind rarely seen in the Korean theater, which foretells the future direction of his works.

Overall, Lee showed interests in society and politics through his work: in *Heojaebi*[35] *nori* (*The Rite of Puppets*), an adaptation of Kantor's *The Dead Class*, and *Faust in Blue Jeans*, which reinterpreted *Faust* from the perspective of a Korean intellectual, he critiqued the despotic power within contemporary Korean society and sense of shame among intellectuals; in *Mask of Fire, King Lear of Our Time*, and *Problematic Man King Yeonsan*, he anatomized the nature of a man in power; and in *The Dummy Bride*, he explores the depravity and salvation of the public. From Lee's political interests, it is sometimes possible to gleam an aspect of him as a critical realist. However, aspects such as the presentation of a destructive and aggressive stage that demolishes the established language of drama, the creation of intense stage imagery, the use of anachronisms, transcendental factors punctuated with political interest, and multifaceted, contradictory and open approach toward humanity, society, history and politics; all of such characteristics render Lee under the category of a postmodernist whose primary talent is to excite and enrapture the audience.

His language as a playwright adds another energizing factor to his plays. Plays written by Lee are filled with intense, solid,

The Dummy Bride
directed by Lee Youn-taek, 1993
(Photo © Theatre Troupe Georipae)

Problematic Man King Yeonsan
directed by Lee Youn-taek, 1995
(Photo © Yoo Theater,
Theatre Troupe Georipae)

inflammatory poetic language in stark contrast to ordinary prose, in testament to his talents as a poet. Also seen in his early work *Citizen K*, this propensity was affected and deepened by his experience of directing Heiner Müller's *Der Auftrag* (The Mission). In short, his language attacks the audience through direct narration by escaping the confines of theatrical dialogue as a passive form of speech. The use of candid language, the resulting characters and the atmosphere of rough ideality and agitation comprise source of his theatrical energy as well as the characteristics of postmodernist drama in the rejection of the values of representation.

Moreover, Lee's interests also extended over the traditional stories and performing art forms of Korea. His 1990 play *Ogu–The Ritual of Death* is the illustration of funerary rites and the eponymous ritual of *ogu-gut* to wish for the living to enjoy heavenly rest in death, employing the scene of a home in mourning to create the Korean sense of a scene of death, in which life and death, tragic solemnity and humor, death and sex, realms of the living and the dead fuse and intertwine. The play realizes a deconstructive worldview that hovers between life and death omnipresent in the Korean conception, perception, and customs of death. In *The Dummy Bride* in 1993, which recounts the death and narrative resurrection of a female street food vendor, Lee aimed to subvert the desolate postmodernist society by introducing the *mireuk*, the transcendent and theological concept as a uniquely Korean

Ogu - The Ritual of Death directed by Lee Youn-taek, 1990 (Photo © Theatre Troupe Georipae)

interpretation of the Buddhist element of Maitreya,[36] in order to break and escape from the closed reality.

As a director, Lee values the inherent potential of performers' body language as much as poetic language. Lee's conception of the performer is not as a mere conduit that delivers the meaning of sentences but as a physical reality, and therefore, the performers are vital in terms of determining the pace, gravitas, and rhythm of his plays. His experiments with a Korean style of physical training centering on breathing techniques and endurance are a part of the efforts towards this end, as with the attempt to generate multifaceted theatrical semiotics such as stage pictures and music. Lee proves himself as a director capable of creating the most shocking and energetic stage today, imagining scenes such as the royal palace collapsing into ruin, and the reed field in which the living and dead ghosts gather to mingle, featured in *Problematic Man King Yeonsan,* which seeks to enter the internal mind of a young king, Yeonsan (r. 1494-1506), known as a tyrant of the Joseon Dynasty; as well as the striking music and the tableau at the scene of the murdered female street vendor as she is resurrected with her baby in *The Dummy Bride.* The farcical vivaciousness in *Ogu–The Ritual of Death* and self-directed humor seen in *Faust in Blue Jeans* are somewhat demonstrative of the lightness of postmodernism.

Chae Seung-hun: Insanity of Death in the Criticism towards Civilization

While Lee Youn-taek swept the theatrical scene in 1990s Seoul with a number of works supported by his popular and onrushing energy, Chae Seung-hun assumes a unique place in the discussion of 1990s theater with his avant-garde rarity and an almost neurotic level of concentration. Despite strong influences by Antonin Artaud, Heiner Müller, and Tadeusz Kantor, Chae localized the influence through his own interpretations. In essence, he was an elitist who pursued artistic purity to the point of abstruseness, but his strong deconstructionist tendencies place him alongside many contemporary artists in skirting the boundary between modernists and postmodernists.

Despite having directed the plays by Eugène Ionesco and Peter Handke since the 1980s, Chae established his reputation as the director of brutality, insanity, and death since directing Artaud's *Les Cenci* (*The Cenci*) in 1990, and Heiner Müller's *Die Hamletmaschine* (*Hamletmachine*), both staged for the first time in Korea. Then, in 1998, he released *A Red Inn Sunk in a Blue Coffin*, an original work that he wrote and directed. Chae's main interest was the barbaric violence repetitively pervading the canon of mainstream history, which led him to reinterpret history from the viewpoint of the public as the victims of the history of violence, in the belief that only death and pain could awaken the public to reflect upon and resist the violence of history.[37] In the course of this project, he mobilized Heiner Müller's reflection on history, Artaud's brutality, and Kantor's thinking about death.

At the same time, however, Chae actively adopted shamanic ritual *gut* as a uniquely Korean theme, in concert with the pace and movement of Asian theater, which are commensurate with Artaud's worldview or expressions. An empty stage, simple objects such as a wooden coffin, extreme transition between stillness and motion, deconstructed language and long silences, brutal displays of violence, the twisted bodies and groans of the actors, distorted movement akin to zombies or marionettes[38] frequently feature as elements in his plays. In *The Cenci*, attention was drawn to the strong lighting and grotesque costumes, such as high-heeled wooden shoes and a golden mask used in the endeavor to overcome the literary aspect of the play while in *Hamletmachine*, the spotlight was reserved for the impactful physicality of the mime artist cast for Hamlet as well as the naked bodies of some performers including the character of Ophelia. In the latter play, Chae refused to remain confined to Müller's original text and instead freely and loosely montaged creative images and fragmentary acts, to shock the audience with appalling scenes within the play such as the pregnant Ophelia writhing in a bathtub with a knife plunged into her stomach.

Chae's original play *A Red Inn Sunk in a Blue Coffin* is set

Hamletmachine directed by Chae Seung-hun, 1990
(Photo © Changpa Theater Company)

A Red Inn Sunk in a Blue Coffin directed by Chae Seung-hun, 1998 (Photo © Changpa Theater Company)

in modern Korea, but expresses the recurring violence and horrors of history. When the play begins at a small studio with seats placed on each side overlooking the stage, the audience is made to endure tens of minutes through a scene of women in the traditional white clothes of the Joseon era, sitting down to face the audience in a pose as if to turn a spinning wheel and instead unrolling toilet papers as slowly as possible. Against the backdrop of the small and haphazard stage setup, this is followed by the entrance of characters who appear to represent figures in Korea's modern history of interference by world powers, and mimes reminding the audience of Koreans throughout history who were pillaged and subjugated. This simple and silent play induced a state of heightened tension and intense concentration among the audience to notice and contemplate even the smallest movements made by performers. Chae continued similar works in the 2000s, and *Dudeuri Dudeuri*, an adaptation of Kantor's *Wielopole Wielopole*, received an assortment of awards and critical acclaim in Japan, Germany, and Romania along with *Hamletmachine*.

Choi Yong-hun's Theater Company ZakEunShinHwa: Exhilarating Satire through Collective Creation

Whereas Lee Youn-taek and Chae Seung-hun began their careers in the 1990s when they were in early 40s, younger directors in their 30s including Choi Yong-hun, Kim Dong-hyun, and Cho Kwang-hwa began to apply their sense of postmodernism in producing innovative works during the same period centering the small-scale theater Hyehwa-dong 1st Number. Foremost among this new generation of directors, Choi Yong-hun founded the theater company ZakEunShinHwa (ZESH)[39] and recruited youthful members to create deconstructive, physical, and experimental works, dedicated to criticizing modern civilization, modern power structures, and political awareness with a cathartic and popular atmosphere, which is in contrast with Chae Seung-hun.

It is often speculated that Choi's works have received influences from the American theater group Open Theater.

His leading production is *War Mu?Sic!* (1990), a localization of *Viet Rock* by Megan Terry of the Open Theater, which he produced through collective creation and using methods consisting of a parallel montage, improvisation, and transformation of the featured episodes. *Viet Rock* satirizes the foolishness and violence of war through episodes surrounding the Vietnam War, and Choi recreated the play as a somewhat localized fable of the more universal theme as conveyed by the original, narrating the experience of a young Korean man as he is forced into war against his will. The sequel *War Mu?Sic! 2* invites episodes of a more mundane nature, featuring subways, video games, Hong Kong movies, TV programs, fast food, and civil defense training.

Magic Eye Scream of 1995 is yet another work of collective creation and improvisation among members of his theatrical

War Mu?sic! directed by Choi Yong-hun, 1990 (Photo © ZakEunShinHwa)

company. This play deploys juxtaposed episodes set on the notoriously hectic Subway Line 2 of the Seoul subway system, depicting the loss of identity and the consequent confusion facing various people in and around the subway line, such as passengers, sellers, vagrants, station employees, and religious fanatics. Choi's novel attempt, namely the method of collective creation to gather young theater members to produce their ideas into a play, and the tendency to accept the fragmentation of life in an adulterated form by translating aspects of modern consumer culture and materialist civilization into episodes in an ordinary, lighter, and cheerful sketch. As a model of emulation for younger theater groups after the 1990s, this stylistic propensity was arguably the postmodernist variation of the more serious efforts towards collaborative creation works, as attempted by Theater Yeonwoo in the 1980s.

Magic Eye Scream directed by Choi Yong-hun, 1995 (Photo © ZakEunShinHwa)

Cho Kwang-hwa: The Patriarchal System and the Opressed Sexual Energy

Cho Kwang-hwa is among the younger generation of playwrights and directors from the 1990s who produced plays filled with spectacles and energy. More active in terms of theatrical writing than directing, he is perhaps unique in the way that he focuses on patriarchal problems within a family and issues among family members, such as an Oedipus complex, incest, male violence, and feminine alternatives rather than social, historical, or ontological issues; and his interests incline towards popular tastes in portraying brutal violence and intense melodrama among family members and nearby individuals.

His reputation in the theatrical circles developed as he published plays such as *A Cat in Jongno* (1992), *A Rainy Season* (1993), and *A Flower Snake Asks to Coil Itself around My Leg* (1995). The subject matters in these plays are recurrent in his later works; an incompetent father oppressing his family and asserting his reign over them, a mother making sacrifices for the family: sons and daughters striving to rebuild the family in the place of their father even at the cost of using violence, deep intimacy between a brother and a sister, and a strong sense of nostalgia towards masculinity.

The Masculine Drive of 1997, which was Cho's first attempt at writing and directing a play, propelled him to stardom in the theatrical world. Subtitled, "The Violent Urge in the Clenched Fists of Sons," this play depicts a male protagonist, Jangjeong, the leader of a minor gang in a small town who worships Al Pacino from the *The Godfather* movie series, as he attempts to lead both his family and his gang, eventually ending in his ruination. In the place of his father, a gambling addict who destroyed the homestead and himself, Jangjeong strives to become the head of the family to provide for his long suffering mother, introverted younger brother Yujeong, and mentally challenged younger sister, Dallae, whom he loves over all else. However, his way of dealing with his family and gang is based on violence as opposed to love. The significance behind

The Masculine Drive directed by Cho Kwang-hwa, 1997
(Photo © Hwang Jae-yeon)

The Masculine Drive is ambivalent: despite criticizing the patriarchal system and male chauvinist violence, the main source of vigor and vitality throughout the entire play is the theme of violence, the powerful fantasy towards masculinity, and the low-brow sensibilities in popular culture that instigates this.[40] *The Masculine Drive* became hugely popular with remarkable acting performance for the characters of Jangjeong, who tightly clutches a Japanese sword as he makes a vow under a large poster of Al Pacino, and the mentally challenged Dallae; the vaudeville performance of the male actors for its effective addition in spite of the limitations of throughlines; the sensationally beautiful tableau of the scene of the murder; and the sexual energy exuding throughout the entire play.

Cho's active contributions continued through the 1990s, producing works ranging from *Ophelia* (1995), which depicts the incestuous love between Ophelia and Laertes as they absurdly fall victim to Hamlet's revenge, to *Mad Kiss* (1998), the story of a love which falls into isolation and severance due to obsessive physical passion, and to *The Iron-faced Buddha*, a sci-fi play and a grand critique of civilization from the Buddhist perspective. Nevertheless, none of his successive works enjoyed as much success as *The Masculine Drive*, and Cho's theatrical energy failed to transition smoothly into the 2000s.

Kim Ara: A Glamorous Stylist amid Nature

Kim Ara has the rare distinction of being a female director and occupying a place in the Korean theatrical circles as a unique stylist. When the 1980s theater was dominated by political drama that lacked aesthetics, Kim made her directorial debut with *A Rose Tattoo* and *Cinders*, notable for staging feminine, energetic, and well-organized performances. She gained recognition for her remarkable directing techniques with *The Captured Soul* (1991) which thrillingly expressed the works of Joseon-era painter Jang Seung-eop using video footage reproducing the movement of a galloping horse on a screen as it follows the artist's brush strokes; and with *As If Seen a Flower in Midwinter*, which mixes the meta-fictional question of "What is an actor?" with traditional folklores to be amalgamated into a comprehensive theater with traditional dances and songs.

In 1992, Kim founded Theater Group Mucheon with the inaugural play *Hidden Water*, which used motions from traditional Korean martial arts to embody the ordeals and the process of overcoming such ordeals in Korean history. Subsequently, she departed the indoor theaters of Daehangno in favor of a theater camp amid the stark nature around the small town of Jukjeon at a two-hour distance from Seoul, going on to stage a succession of Shakespearean plays armed with her own baroque style, such as *Human Lear* and *Hamlet*

Hamlet Project (1999, upper) and *A Song of Mandala* (2007, lower)
directed by Kim Ara (Photo © Theater Group Mucheon)

Project. From the 2000s, she began showing interest in silence performance and site-specific performance, which are generally staged near historic sites of significance to the play. She drew international attention by staging *Dear River* in 2006 near the Han River, and the 2007 performance *A Song of Mandala*, staged in Angkor Wat to commemorate the spirits of those sacrificed in the killing fields.

Her works, especially those of the 1990s, feature flamboyant baroque-style costumes and surreal imagery, and energetic music and sound effects, prominently featuring percussion, electronic music, *pansori*, and improvised piano performance. For the creation of motions harmonious to the aforementioned facets, she adopted the energetic movement of traditional martial arts, such as *taekkyeon*[41] and *subyeokchigi*.[42] Her theatrical work of this time is designated by herself as a multi-genre musical theater. After she entered into nature in Jukjeon, her Shakespearean plays became more deconstructive and showed a greater tendency towards performance art. Surrounded by the roughness of nature exposed upon the red soil, mounds of earth, water, and sewage pipes occupy the space as if comprising some kind of installation art, while the performers scattered across the stage use wireless microphones to utter language detached from meaning, or to hum, or to merely stand in silence. Hamlet is construed as a man with disability who cannot move away from a pond, while the ghost of the dead king appears on an excavator, King Lear's two evil daughters are expressed as three separate beings representing sex, power, and futility, and Cordelia remains silent and only animated by her humming. Costumes worn by the performers remain in the exaggerated baroque style costumes, while the hollowness of their inner side is reflected through the video on the external screen as they suffer from the discordant nature of desires. Even the moon shrouded behind the clouds could comprise a part of the performance. Comprehensive performance within nature closely resembles a *gut*, or a ritual, rather than a play, as human beings beg for salvation from mankind's limitations and suffering amidst the nakedness of nature. Indeed, Kim asserts that her ultimate pursuit is to create a ritual. It is likely that this theatrical philosophy is the motivational factor behind her penchant for producing performances of a massive scale, which exclude elements of theatrical fiction under the shadow of ancient civilizations inherent in the historical sites used as theatrical venues.

Oh Tae-suk: Exposé on the Inhumanity of Korean Society

While adhering to his own theatricality, Oh Tae-suk became more interested in social and political criticism in the 1990s after the demise of military dictatorship. His main concern was the loss of pride and integrity among Koreans regarding the past, and the corrupting influences of capitalist and

Why Did Sim Cheong Plunge into the Indang Sea Twice?
directed by Oh Tae-suk, 1994 (Photo © Mokwha Repertory Company)

mammonistic society. Such concerns were initially reflected in *Vinyl House* (1989) which gruesomely depicts Koreans who are tamed in a controlled society like plants in a greenhouse. In his subsequent play *Why Did Sim Cheong Plunge into the Indang Sea Twice?* (1990), he denounces the dehumanization of Korean society at the time with greater ferocity. The play borrows the motif of the traditional novel *Simcheongjeon* (The Story of Sim Cheong), in which Sim Cheong sacrifices herself by jumping into the sea to restore her blind father's sight. The play features the scene of a potent warning to the greedy and the egocentric, when Sim Cheong, returns from the underwater palace of the Dragon King only to drown herself along with the women who are forced into prostitution as victims of human trafficking after failing to pay their ransom; although this scene is broadcast live on TV, it fails to draw any kind of response from the citizens watching. Another scene that is certain to create a lasting impression of horrifying captivation in the mind of the audience is the one in which a naïve and young country man is broken down by the heartlessness and desolation of the city, scarred with burns over his entire body and made to wear a white mask while he is struck with balls as a human target in an amusement park, his body flailing like a dance and spraying blood-like fluid over the audience.

Oh's 1998 play *A Prisoner of a Thousand Years* shed new light on the recent emergence of terrorists in Korea's modern history. For Oh, terrorists do not necessarily bear a negative connotation. He makes no significant distinctions between Ahn Jung-geun who resisted the occupation of Korea by assassinating a notorious Japanese Prime Minister; Ahn Doo-hee who assassinated the beloved post-liberation politician and nationalist Kim Koo; soldiers who fired upon innocents in the Gwangju Democratization Movement; or Kim Jae-gyu, who killed Park Chung-hee. Oh's perspective is that such figures were merely individuals who were unsuccessful in finding true leaders and suffered through turbulent times.

A Prisoner of a Thousand Years directed by Oh Tae-suk, 1998
(Photo © Mokwha Repertory Company)

His nostalgia is instead directed towards true human beings, and the past when the concept of "guru" had existed as figures of respect. He yearns for now-absent figures of honorable Koreans, national leaders, and the *paterfamilias*. In this regard, Oh's highly postmodernist inclination in stage production stands in contrast to his substantive aspects as a traditional, romantic, and conservative nationalist.

Bellflower in 1994 depicts the chaos in the late Joseon period as the Korean Empire became subjugated by Japan. Following the failure of the Gapsin Coup in 1884, pro-Japanese reformist Kim Ok-gyun left Korea to wander abroad, only to be killed in a Shanghai hotel by Hong Jong-woo, an emissary of King Gojong. Among the young aristocrats who travelled to the Hague to deliver a secret message from King Gojong to call for the liberation of the Korean Empire, Lee Jun was unable to control his anger upon the failure of his mission and stabbed himself to death on the site. Oh interprets all of these deaths as the sacrifice and struggle of the public in the absence of a true leader, the true paternal figure to guide the nation during times of tumult.

Kosovo, and Diaspora in 1999 identifies parallels between the suffering among Albanians during the civil war and the traumatic experience of the Korean War. In addition, Oh continued to pursue his works with passion throughout the 1990s, and produced a wide range of controversial plays: creating a farcical depiction of the memories and scars of an old war widow in *Unsanggak Tower* (1990); resolving the grudges of ancient kings of rival kingdoms through a village *gut* in *Moonlight over the Baekma River* (1993); and projecting his own tastes in directing *Romeo and Juliet* and *Die Dreigroschenoper* (*The Threepenny Opera*).

Moonlight over the Baekma River directed by Oh Tae-suk, 1993
(Photo © Mokwha Repertory Company)

Sohn Jin-chaek: National Consciousness and Advanced Theatrical Aesthetics

Sohn Jin-chaek's determination behind leaving the Theatre Group Minye, and newly establishing the Michoo Theatre Company was due to his belief that Minye's works had become complacent in its direct and fragmentary adoption of traditional dances, songs, and motifs, which was anachronistic in responding to the contemporary sensibilities of the modern audience. It was potentially for this reason that Sohn strived to develop contemporary characteristics while retaining the traditional code in his works of the 1990s.

In 1991, the play *The Shadow of Time* was produced through the collaboration of three intellectuals; German playwright and director Manuel Lutgenhorst who travelled the world in admiration of the Orient, liberal Eastern philosopher Kim Yong-ok of Korea, and Sohn Jin-chaek, who was in pursuit of a truly novel and Korean method of expression. The play can be described as a collection of typical postmodernist scenes, such as "modern meditation music and the rhythms of traditional *sanjo* (free-style solo); rolling shadows on the screen projection as an allusion to genesis; the deliberate appearance of an old ascetic and a young monk, said to represent Lao-tzu and Plato; characters dressed in *hanbok* whose silhouettes stir in the headlights of LeMans and Elantra automobiles; recent student demonstrations shown through projector slides; flowing lectures by Kim Yong-ok, known as Doal, or To-ol by his nom de plume; and the sporadic insertion of wild dance choreographies."[43] However, the excessively radical and experimental content and form of the execution of the play did not garner a positive response overall.

Written by Yun Dae-seong and directed by Sohn in 1993, *The Sky of Namsadang*[44] depicts the life of Baudeogi, a legendary figure who led the male-only travelling theatrical troupe *namsadang*, and as a result, the play prominently features the *namsadang's samulnori* (traditional percussion quartet) and acrobatics such as tightrope walking, while creating a sense of a surrealist spectacle in the overall imagery at the same time.

That, Fire in 1999, written by Kim Yong-ok and directed by Sohn, depicts the history of potters in the Sim Su-gwan family, and the stubborn pride that lasted over the 15 generations since Sim was taken to Japan four centuries ago. The history of potters is expressed with intense imagery and grandiose material density through the various theatrical representation of pottery production and the physical movements of characters of the Sim family, which traverse through time and space. Situated between the audience and the stage, the orchestra pit was converted to represent the pottery kiln, from the depths of which flared light as if from live flames. Moreover, the vibrations from the "kiln" occupied a low pitched frequency, thereby stimulating the tactile sensation all

The Sky of Namsadang diredted by Sohn Jin-chaek, 1993 (Photo © Michoo Theatre Company)

over the body rather than the audience's sense of hearing.

Although Michoo Theatre Company's works of the 1990s maintained the sense of national identity and pride in terms of selection of works and planning, and at the same time, attempted to adapt advanced forms of stage expression, the shortcomings of the first two attempts resulted in the failure to establish a significant presence. The importance of Sohn's leadership over Michoo in the 1990s proved more evident than ever by introducing Chilean playwright Ariel Dorfman's *Death and the Maiden* and *The Other Side*, or through *madang nori*, which had enjoyed commercial popularity during traditional holidays and year-end festivities since the 1980s. *Madang nori* had gained tremendous popularity for more than 20 years by generating a popular interpretation of the form of *madanggeuk*, and satire and humor in relation to contemporary society, but was unsuccessful in receiving high praise in terms of theatrical aesthetics due to its lack of a deeper level of thought and overt reliance upon the improvisational witticisms of its stars and simplistic staging of spectacles to entertain the audience. However, *madang nori* remains noteworthy for facilitating the succession of traditional performing arts, postmodernist performance, and studies of audience and culture.

Ki Kook-seo: Scumbags of Postmodernist Society

Having begun the 1990s with an intensive array of productions, Ki Kook-seo of Theater Company 76 entered a hiatus from creation activities. Followed on from his works of the 1980s, *Hamlet IV* and *Hamlet V* of 1990 saw a more radical degree of deconstruction in relation to the original plays. Instead of external conflicts such as the struggle against dictatorial regimes, Ki employed an amplified sense of self-consciousness and elements of theatrical experimentation to expose the festering wounds that pervaded society in 1990s Korea, depicting the lingering effects of the Gwangju massacre perpetrated under Chun Doo-hwan's Fifth Republic, repeated incidents of death by torture and public security crises, and despair entertainment culture consisting of sex, sports, and pornography. *Hamlet IV* is made up of three parts: Part I features the scene of a "rehearsal" in order to demolish any illusions towards the theatrical art form; Part II presents assorted episodes of lethargy and hopelessness, such as the experiences of Hamlet as a young man living in modern-day Korea as he undergoes encounters with the dead, love, violence, sex, drugs, the confessions of torturers, and an interview scene reminiscent of the TV show *Johnny Yoon Show*; while every deceased character is brought back to life in Part III to remind the audience that the experience is merely a work of theater. Although *Hamlet V* does not differ substantively from *Hamlet IV*, it is more liberal in its inclusion of profanities, explicit jokes, and political criticism.

Miari Texas, written and directed by Ki in the same year, was a controversial play that indicated the advent of a new theatrical wave of domestic realism. The work represents the hyper-realistic portrayal of young prostitutes, pimps, and lowlifes who lead parasitic lives in a red-light district. The play deviates from the spectacles of 1990s theater, instead choosing to remain free of any theatrical form, featuring characters without motives, aims, or consistent personalities as if existing on stage by coincidence to narrate mundane daily lives and meaningless chatter. At times, Ki appeared on the stage himself, playing a minor role in his ordinary sloppy attire.

The Zippies (1990) has a similar atmosphere. Though it was released as a joint production by an external writer and Theater Company 76, the overall influence from Ki's style is unmistakable. The play enacts the story of a background actor, an unsuccessful film director, a beggar, an ex-convict as their paths cross on the late-night subway. As the group bands together to produce a work of amateur pornography, the rest of their time is spent in ceaseless and disjointed chatter, exchanging cheesy jokes, phony anecdotes, wordplay, and vulgar stories. This novel yet bleak perspective allows a glimpse into the slice-of-life drama of the company, which is continued by Park Keun-hyeong through the 2000s in a more definitive form using the family unit as the basic medium.

05

Appreciation of New Everyday Life and the Search for Alternatives since the 2000s

From the onset of the 1997 financial crisis, the cultural world was not safe in escaping the adverse side-effects of the economic downturn. Entering into the 2000s, hollow postmodernist spectacles disappeared, and the theatrical circles once more saw plays that dealt with daily hardships and problems of reality. A new trend emerged as the exaggerated entertainment in postmodernism gradually established a consistent code to the point of tedium among the audience. Plays that returned to the fundamentals of language and text emerged on the stage to depict daily life in the smallest details, and at the center of the trend was a directorial rookie in his 40s, Park Keun-hyeong. Mainly through the deconstruction of the family, Park addressed the collapse of existing order and values in society, and the overall tone of his plays were based on realism, and yet punctuated with irregular protrusions of oppressed fantasies and rage. During the 2000s, theatrical circles were heavily influenced by postmodernist theater of a style similar to Park's work. Although outspoken political ideology had nearly disappeared from theater, subjects such as the intricate system of oppression and inequality of wealth under the neoliberal economy became the focus of the suppressed rage among young directors.

This new trend is consolidated by similar works of Kim Han-gil, Jang Woo-jae, Choi ZinA, and Yun Yeong-sun. These directors share a common theme in revealing the hidden side behind the appearance of tranquility in daily life, circuitously criticizing social oppression and introducing postmodern or deconstructionist perspectives at unexpected intervals while generally maintaining the representational aspect towards life. On the contrary, Han Tae-sook, Koh Sun-woong, and Choi Chi-eon follow in the footsteps of Kim Ara and Cho Kwang-hwa of the 1990s, marking their place in Korean theater with intensely vibrant productions that emphasize the body, use of imagery, and physicality. The common proclivity among this group of directors is the emphasis on the physicality (*korperlichkeit*) of the performers as the source of theatrical energy, but materials such as water and soil are occasionally utilized to stimulate the bodies and senses of the audience.

Following the 1990s, the process of adapting Shakespearean plays with modern, deconstructive, and Korean attributes accelerated as a trend, which was joined by not only Lee Youn-taek, Kim Ara, Cho Kwang-hwa, Ki Kook-seo, but also Oh Tae-suk, Han Tae-sook, Yang Jeong-woong, Park Keun-hyeong, and Koh Sun-woong. Oh Tae-suk's *Romeo and Juliet* and *Tempest*, Han Tae-sook's *Lady Macbeth*, Yang Jeong-woong's *A Midsummer Night's Dream*, and Koh Sun-woong's

Killbeth were widely introduced to the world as representative works among post-2000s theater. In addition, the introduction of foreign experimental theater to local theatrical festivals in Korea vitalized the sensibilities of young theatrical people and raised the standard of appreciation among local audiences.

As mainstream playwright-directors such as Oh Tae-suk and Lee Youn-taek became less active in producing plays, the spectrum of theatrical works began to diversify in the 2000s. For example, Yang Jeong-woong is known both domestically and internationally as a director of cosmopolitan taste, challenging the global theater scene by recreating Western classics into a Korean style. Non-verbal performances that have garnered international acclaim as to be invited to theatrical festivals worldwide include Sadari Movement Lab's *Woyzeck*, whose set consists only of a number of chairs, and *Nanta*, which uses only kitchenware and percussion instruments for the performance. Choi ZinA, unlike the elaborate theatricalism demonstrated by other female directors, such as Han Tae-sook and Kim Ara, attracted attention by highlighting issues in female identity and independence within the context of the calmness of daily life. In addition, Oh Tae-suk and Bae Sam-sik are producing works that address universal issues of the new millennium, such as the ecosystem or the question of life.

Park Keun-hyeong: Cracks underneath the Surface of Ordinary Life

Park Keun-hyeong made his debut with *Chunhyang 1991*, a modernized and cynical dramatization of one of the most well-known classical novels in Korea, which was staged in the Theater Company 76, founded by Ki Kook-seo. His debut was followed by collaborative creation with members of the Theater Company 76, producing works such as *The Zippies* and *Aspirin*, which depict the despair of daily life in contemporary Korea. In addition, Park wrote and directed plays such as *Dumplings* and *Mice*, which shows the bizarre appetites of an impoverished family.

In 1999, Park began to gain attention of the theatrical world with *The Ode to Youth*, a nonchalant portrayal of the destroyed hierarchy of a family. Having founded the Golmokgil Theatre Company in 2001, Park went on to publish a succession of controversial works, such as *Generation after Generation, Kyung Sook, Kyung Sook's Father*, and *Don't Get Too Shocked* that convey the incomprehensible nature and the conflicts of daily life within a family, which established Park as one of the most important playwrights in contemporary Korean theater.

His formula to popular interest included a number of elements. First is the restoration of the mundane. The previous generation of theatrical leaders in the 1990s were Oh Tae-suk, Lee Youn-taek, Cho Kwang-hwa, and Kim Ara, most

Kyung Sook, Kyung Sook's Father directed by Park Keun-hyeong, 2006
(Photo © Golmokgil Theatre Company)

of whose plays started from grandiose discourses, such as tradition or mythology, thereby strongly conveying sensual and formalist aspects, as well as abstract and ideal inclinations. In contrast, Park returned aspects of actual daily life onto the stage. Naturally, everyday life of the 1990s differed from that of past trends of theatrical spectacle. Our lives, language, and behavior are no longer constrained by logical causality, and even though ordinary life may maintain superficial resemblance to the past, the similarity is merely a thin veneer that conceals the great underlying emotions of madness, anger, and cynicism.

Second is Park's distinct sense of theatrical grammar. The uniqueness of his plays has a delicate flavor to the degree that is hard to define in a word. To borrow existing concepts, Park's plays contain elements of minimalism, hyper-realism, and fantastic realism, which invite the association with Harold Pinter or Sam Shepard. In most cases, his plays open in an empty or dilapidated space with a few, mundane props, instantly entering into a simple dramatic situation through the simplest of lines or actions by a limited number of performers. Though appearing highly realistic at the same time, the featured dramatic scene is intertwined with gruesome illusions or almost grotesque unpredictability, through which Park navigates casually and brazenly as to border on indifference. He is unshakable in his composure, while his rebellious side exudes through the indifference underlying his whimsical humor. Park's quiet rebelliousness is the manifestation of the nightmares created by the post-industrial society beyond the level of the family unit, such as the lives that are discarded like garbage, the reality of the divided nation that has since become the accepted norm, and the paralysis of historical awareness.

The third merit of Park's plays is his passionate interest in the lives of human beings, which had been gradually fading from Korean theater. It would not be an exaggeration to claim that it was difficult to encounter humanity in Korean theater of the 1990s. Too often, the human aspect was concealed behind a pretense of sensibilities or translated into lifeless performance semiotics. In Park's drama, however, it was at least possible to detect a level of passion towards life. Recurrent in his early productions, such as *Mice* and *Dumplings*, the motifs of meals and abnormal appetites are allegorical for the desperate struggle for survival, whereas his interest in the family as a unit and the basis of his plays constitutes the effort to maintain the minimum relationship necessary to live a life worthy of human dignity. At times, his portrait of a distorted family takes place within a more detailed historical context against the twisted history of modern Korea. In *The Ode to Youth*, which earned him a critical reputation, a high school student and his father drink *soju* together with instant noodles for a snack; the father visits and asks for money from his ex-

The Ode to Youth directed by Park Keun-hyeong, 2007
(Photo © Golmokgil Theatre Company)

Don't Get Too Shocked directed by Park Keun-hyeong, 2006
(Photo © Golmokgil Theatre Company)

wife, whom he blinded and forced to work as a masseuse; and the son brings home an older, epileptic barmaid to settle as a family in a single-room flat. *Generation after Generation* is the satirical saga of the paltry ways in which a family has endured through the generations, from the chaotic aftermath of liberation from Japanese rule, through conscription in the Vietnam War, through to the present day.

Since the 2000s, Park has often dealt with the irresponsibility or absence of a father from his traditional role as the breadwinner of a family. *Kyung Sook, Kyung Sook's Father* illustrates a selfish and incompetent father from the daughter's perspective against the backdrop of turbulent events in the modern history of Korea, such as the Japanese occupation of Korea and the Korean War, while *Don't Get Too Shocke*d narrates the story of a woman who enters into prostitution at a karaoke bar while living with her father-and brother-in-law instead of her husband, who left home to become a movie director. As soon as the performance begins, the father-in-law is seen having hung himself in a bathroom, neither alive nor dead, while her autistic brother-in-law maintains a relationship of sexual ambiguity with her, and she herself brings a client home and encounters her husband as he returns from his long absence. This may be indicative of a shift in the focus of Park's plays, from the absence of a *paterfamilias* to the female members of a family. Possessing a remarkable capacity as an acting trainer, Park maintains a strong sense of fellowship with the actors and actresses of his theatrical company Golmokgil, and draws many aspects of his drama from their life experiences and spontaneous responses. His performers adeptly convey the hyper-realist acting characteristic of Park, which suppresses an inner neurosis under a layer of sly humor, whereas the audience responds with dumbfounded laughter and inner fever to the bizarre subversions and irony that unfold without any hesitation under the guise of daily life.

Han Tae-sook: Mise-en-scène of Dark Desire

Han Tae-sook is among the few female playwright-directors in the theatrical circles of the 1990s Korea, along with Kim Ara, and one of few theater artists capable of filling large-scale theaters. Contrary to Kim Ara, who endeavored to escape the confines of the theatrical stage, Han devotes herself to stage aesthetics and the establishment of images, using creative paintings and intense energy to guide her stage direction. These characteristics are only embodied through thorough perfectionism and high standards of completion in her works, which distinguish themselves from most others in light of the prevalence of amateurism and mediocrity in Korean theater.

Han's stages are also notable for the dark and negative atmosphere. To the extent that someone even called her "satanic aestheticist," behind the external surface of splendor and aesthetical refinement indwell gruesome malice, feeling of guilt, despondency, and shadows of distorted human relations. Her plays often feature tensions from the juxtaposition of beauty and ugliness, delicateness and strength, masculinity and femininity, morality and brutality. At the center of her play is always a female character. Han's perspective on femininity and masculinity, however, is highly complex. At times, a female character hides her inner masculinity, while sometimes femininity is found within masculinity. She has even been known to change the sex or gender of characters in her productions.

Han's productions are characterized by her focus on sensuousness and materiality, and the energy that permeates the stage. On her stage, live music features frequently while stage props are replaced by an abundance of works by sculptors; in a similar manner, thematic significance is illustrated with objects, materials like ice, water, and mud, or grotesque creatures instead of language. Occasionally, Han sets up steeply-inclined walls or drills a sizeable hole on the stage floor. Such sensual objects, materials, and spaces overwhelm any form of semantic signs in creating the sense of energy enough to fill the entire stage, and presenting the audience with an unforgettable experience.

Han, who had refrained from production for a long time since her debut with *Dutchman* in 1978, returned to the stage with the depiction of the love-hate relationship between two sisters in *What Ever Happened to Baby Jane?* Following on, she worked continuously with playwright Jeong Bok-geun in dramatizing the complex mentality of women in crisis. Their collaborative works include *Princess Deokhye* (1995), depicting of the tragic story of a princess in late Joseon Dynasty, along with *A Face Behind a Face* (1996), and *I, Kim Su-im* (1997), which dramatized the incident of female spy Kim Su-im.

The work that helped her establish a solid position was the 1999 adaptation of *Lady Macbeth*. Focusing on the desire and guilt of the titular character as she manipulates her

Lady Macbeth directed by Han Tae-sook, 1999 (Photo © Lim-AMC)

weak-willed husband into murder and power struggle, Lady Macbeth explores her dark inside with the minor character of a court physician. However, Han replaces her inner desire not with reproductive acts but with materials such as mud, ice, and water, or direct objects, such as the performer's body and songs. The performance of Seo Joo-hee (Lady Macbeth) and her strong physicality, supported by the material struggle of object artist Lee Yeong-ran, musicians and singers who fill the stage during the scene of a nightmare, the sex scene in which Lady Macbeth mounts and dominates Macbeth, all of such factors contributed to making this production Han's representative work by adding her unique intense color to the performance. To date, this play has been staged many times in Korea and

Killbeth directed by Koh Sun-woong, 2010 (Photo © Play Factory Mabangzen)

abroad, for example, the 2002 staging in Poland and on the eve before the commencement of the 2008 Beijing Summer Olympics.

Killbeth, by the young director Koh Sun-woong, is also noteworthy as a play that deconstructs *Macbeth* with as much energy as Han Tae-sook. The English title *Killbeth* is a twist on words in keeping with its Korean title *Kallomakbeseu*, which is a pun conjoining the name Macbeth with the Korean phrase "to slash indiscriminately with a sword," representing the strength, energy, and unique rhythms of medieval swordsmen through the performance. This excessive masculine energy is no less than the materialization of Macbeth's inordinate desire for power. Understandably, certain commentary highlighted the simplicity of this reinterpretation, which nevertheless gathered strong popularity in China and other countries.

Lady Macbeth by Han Tae-sook was followed by the 2003 release of *A Train for Xian*, which was also written and directed by Han. *A Train for Xian* explores the theme of male homosexuality, which had remained a subject of discomfort for Korean theater yet. Through the scene of a rattling train carriage bound for the Chinese city of Xian, Han juxtaposes a sculptor's homosexual obsession that drives him to taxidermy

A Train for Xian directed by Han Tae-sook, 2003 (Photo © Lim-AMC)

his lover and the desire for immortality displayed by China's first emperor Qin Shi Huang as he built the mausoleum containing the terracotta army. The two desires meet through a life-sized clay sculpture, and in fact, the final scene of the play fills the stage with full-scale male statues made by sculptor Lim Ok-sang.

Han's later works continued to modernize classics through *A Hunchback Richard III* (2004), *Iago and Othello* (2006), and *Oedipus* (2011). *A Hunchback Richard III* in which actor Ahn Seok-hwan occupied the title role to demonstrate a bizarre energy of feminine madness on the steep slope created on the stage; *Iago and Othello*, which replaced Iago's dark inner side with the allegorical image of a black dog; *Oedipus*, a production commemorating the reestablishment of the National Theater Company of Korea, which emphasized the visual effects of the chorus who were suspended from an elevated slope; and the recent works *Antigone* and *The Divine Comedy* which presented vertical interpretations of heaven and the underworld. Criticisms towards Han's work opine that her interpretive perspective is somewhat equivocal, but her mise-en-scène and visual images are provocative enough to overwhelm such criticism and even the audience.

Choi ZinA: A Woman as the Subject of Desire

In the 1980s, the wave of feminist theater in Korea briefly attracted housewives as audiences. However, perhaps as feminism as a perspective began to lose ground in Korea and abroad, feminist works of theater became rare despite the fact that the majority of theater audiences in Korea consisted of young women. Works of Choi ZinA, who was in her 30s when she made her debut as a playwright and director, reveals in a natural fashion many characteristics of feminist poetics or feminist writing and production as identified by scholars in women's studies. Moreover, Choi's plays are exceedingly performative. She does not depend on existing frameworks or structures, instead creating such aspects herself in the process of production without obsessing over the state of completion, while leading the bodies of the performers to move with her and whispering into the ear of the audience to seduce them in a dance. Choi ZinA has many facets in common with Park Keun-hyeong: her writing is performative as if a living creature; on the surface, she depicts simple daily lives; and she harbors a rebellious desire for the subversion of reality. But whereas Park is dark, cynical, and heavily suppressed, Choi is bright, positive, and open in terms of emotions.

One of the distinguishing characteristics Choi's plays have is the progression through a free first-person narrative of a female protagonist. *Not a Love Story* is the story about a female employee at an insurance company who strives to live independently. The young woman's struggle to survive the harsh world freely crosses the boundaries between reality, several layers of unrealities, in addition to time and space. *Not a Love Story* is extraordinary for its nonchalant connections in a comic structure, and the intermittent interjection of meta-theatrical commentary and provocations of physicality.

Love, So Noble and Pure is noteworthy in the way that it addresses a woman as the main agent of physical desire. The tangle of romantic relationships between four characters also develops in the hidden first-person narrative of the female protagonist Seong-hui, and as with Choi's previous work, other characters casually break into Seong-hui's daydreaming, illusions, fantasies, and monologues. *Bless Her* is short and obvious and cheerful. Although sex is not explicitly brought to the surface as in *Love, So Noble and Pure*, few theatrical works can match *Bless Her* in terms of honesty and vivaciousness in describing the female desires. The desire felt by Seon-yeong, who loves her husband but wants a young, exciting lover, is also described in a first-person narrative, but in a more romantic, or more ontological, but more lighthearted and cheerful way than her previous work.

Choi's writing, which mostly focused on desire and love between a man and a woman, began expanding its range gradually in terms of motifs and perspectives. *Unexpected*, detailing a journey to Vietnam uses the mundane subject

Not a Love Story directed by Choi ZinA, 2004 (Photo © Theatre Nolddang)

of overseas travel to describe a peculiar relationship of interdependence. Su-jeong, who leaves on a trip alone to forget the suicide of her friend, returns to Korea having shared many experiences and taken on a little more pain after meeting a Spanish man living in London and a number of Vietnamese acquaintances. The merit of this play is in avoiding the subjective risk of overseas travel to objectify others, instead allowing the Vietnamese innkeepers or street vendors, mountain tribes, and other locals to voice their perspectives in a pluralist mixture. The capacity for good will and bad intentions is not reserved solely for the relatively wealthy traveler Su-jeong, but also shared by the Vietnamese as well. In the end, the play offers unforgettable scenes such as that Su-jeong swaps her clothes under the moonlight with those of a Vietnamese woman selling tropical fruit and that

she dances in melancholy with a Western traveler who could and could not communicate with her.

In her most recent work *House Number 1-28, Cha-sook's* (2010), Choi's performative tendencies are evident. The drama deals with the "process" of building a shabby house in a rural area for 40 days. While building the house, its blueprint changes, the foundation sinks, and even the owner of a part of the land interferes in the work, resulting in the house being left incomplete. But the experience Choi wants to share is not any dramatic incident, crisis or conflict. It is the "process" of building a house, delicate contemplation of the process, and thoughts of sand, pebbles, water, and wind that constitute a house, uniting the audience in a shared experience and thought.

House Number 1-28, Cha-sook's directed by Choi ZinA, 2010 (Photo © Theatre Nolddang)

Bae Sam-sik: Contemplation on Ecological Life

Bae Sam-sik is a welcome figure in Korean theater, which has few playwrights with both depth of thinking and dramaturgy. He shows off a lot of energy to produce not only plays but also *madanggeuk*, adaptation and dramatization of novels, musicals, and *changgeuk*. His solid language and skilled storytelling earned him a reputation through *A Barbarian Woman Ongnyeo* which translates *Ballad for Byeongangsoe*, a *pansori* famous for its rich description of sexual relations between a man and a woman as the persistence of fate; and *Chronicle of a Blood Merchant*, an adaptation of a Chinese novel. *A Fairy in the Wall* in 2005 is a monodrama of Kim Seong-nyeo, who acted in 32 different roles, and depicts the life of a woman who suffered the pain of Korea's modern history. Though the play is an adaptation of an original Japanese novel, it proved Bae's potential as a professional playwright capable of capturing the audience's attention.

Bae started gaining attention not only as a skilled storyteller but also as a controversial playwright with his 2006 production *Jugong Haengjang* (*A Tale of Mr. Jugong*),[45] directed by Sohn Jin-chaek. This play, which presents the life of a drunk under the ban on drinking implemented by King Yeongjo of Joseon Dynasty, expresses the idea that inebriation is not much different from creativity or freedom, through a structure both light and relaxed as the premise, which subtly and boldly

A Fairy in the Wall directed by Sohn Jin-chaek, 2005 (Photo © Michoo Theatre Company)

reveals Bae's potential for creativity. The potential catharsis of this play is continued by *Yeolha Ilgi Manbo* (*Travels in Jehol Province*) directed by Sohn Jin-chaek. This play reconstitutes the travelling diary of Joseon-era scholar Park Ji-won titled *Yeolha Ilgi* (*The Jehol Journal*) through the notion of Gilles Deleuze's creation, desire, escape, and the nomad, resulting in a large-scale production combining abstract imagination and theatrical entertainment to the point of chaos, which drew the criticism for his excessive ideality.

Directed by Kim Dong-hyun in 2008, *White Cherry* was an excellent production subtly presenting the solidarity of life that connects humans with animals, plants, and even fossils, using the backdrop of a rural family and acquaintances, which inspired warm sympathy for life, careful thought of life and time, reflection and humor on daily lives. Also directed by Kim Dong-hyun, *The Bee* (2011) shows a similar theme to *White Cherry*. In *The Bee*, humans, insects, and plants boldly

Jugong Haengjang directed by Sohn Jin-chaek, 2006
(Photo © Michoo Theatre Company)

White Cherry directed by Sohn Jin-chaek, 2008
(Photo © Yonhap News)

generate a consistent inner flow, going as far as to feature a scene of interspecies kissing. The female protagonist On Ga-hui, who is diagnosed with cancer, becomes a queen bee whose nuptial flight coincides with an attempt to win a man's heart. The cancer cells within her body may be a type of virus for bees, while her body, which is eaten away by the cancer cells, becomes a sanctuary of recovery for other bees. Although mankind accepts the expiration of life, it is merely an infinitesimal part of the large scale of time, which flows with unperceivable slowness.

Oh Tae-suk: From Rage and Nightmares to Reconciliation and Life

The 2000s saw Oh Tae-suk beginning to tentatively shift the focus of his interests. His past works outwardly demonstrated cheerful, entertaining, and vibrant theatrical language, which stood in contrast to the dark and negative content such as the painful memories of war or the dehumanization of modern Korea. Now entering his 60s, Oh has begun to place his interests to new and positive aspects including life and the ecosystem. He now forgives and reconciles the pain, agony and rage of the past, and has turned his attention to the preciousness of life and the value of nature and the environment.

The interest Oh has shown in life and the ecosystem since the 2000s can be explained more than easily with the fact that he frequently presents animals as significant beings in his works. In *Love with a Fox*, he weaves the story of foxes extinct in Korea being imported from the Yanbian region of China, projected with the story of building a memorial hall for the Joseon expatriate poet Yun Dong-ju; In *A Centipede and an Earthworm*, he excoriates pollution, the inter-Korean divide, and resolving the lingering issue of collaborators in the Japanese occupation, using the pollution-free animals of a centipede and an earthworm to depict the hellish reality of black market organ sales; In *My Love DMZ*, a number of animals such as a pony, a fox, and a badger appear to protect the ecosystem of the demilitarization zone between the two Koreas; *Galmeori*[46] illustrates a situation in which seniors in the rural area of Galmeo-ri serve as guide dogs in essence, in order to raise funds for their village; in *Bukcheong*[47] *Lion Dance*, timely interest in the animal slaughter stemming from the outbreak of foot and mouth disease meets with animal characters from traditional entertainment such as a lion, a tiger, and a monkey. Among recent, and unstaged plays, *The Rise and Fall of Arungguji*[48] represents an earthworm as a spirit to guard a naïve man who tries to protect the ecosystem of rural areas; *Yonghosangbak* (*A Fight of a Tiger and a Dragon*) addresses a conflict between humans and a tiger which grants prosperity to the village and at the same time poses a threat; in *A Promise to Live Happily Ever After* which depicts the Korean War and the separation between the two Koreas, a mouse appears as an important motif.

In the adaptations of Shakespeare's *Romeo and Juliet* and *Tempest*, animals do not appear as being important in a direct way, but in the course of reconstituting and staging original plays, Oh's interest in life and the ecosystem is partly or explicitly revealed. In *Romeo and Juliet*, he does not directly present animals, but the interpretation of the play's theme and performance invokes the vigor of animals as an allegory. Oh reinterprets the original play about love and frustration of a young boy and girl as the juxtaposition of life versus violence,

1 *Yonghosangbak* (2005)
2 *Bukcheong Lion Dance* (2011)
3 *Romeo and Juliet* (1995)
4 *Tempest* (2010)
directed by Oh Tae-suk (Photo © Mokwha Repertory Company)

and life versus death. The play makes various uses of animal metaphor and metonymy in expressing the energy and vibrant youthfulness of the young lovers before they are forced into violent deaths.

Oh depicted Miranda of *Tempest* as a girl who is full of life and roughly frolicking in nature rather than a beautiful white woman untainted by civilization. The island in which diverse animals live in harmony with humans makes an impression of a community of life cohabited by various living creatures including humans, animals, shamans, unknown beings, rather than original play's dichotomy of humans and animals, good and evil, beauty and ugliness, rulers and subjects. Their innocent vitality brings the warmth of life to reconciliation and forgiveness, the theme of this play and also the area of Oh's recent interests. *Tempest* was officially invited to the Edinburgh International Festival in 2011 to a favorable response.

Lee Youn-taek: Renewed Interpretation of
Koreans throughout History

The intense theatricality and eclecticism of Lee Youn-taek as a director and playwright continued throughout the 2000s. Constantly based on the critical mindset and self-awareness of an intellectual, Lee revealed his inexorable passion for the recurrent themes of interest from his early days, such as the task of inheriting the tradition of Korean entertainment, encountering the masses through musicals and *changgeuk*, creating Korean adaptations of Western classics ranging from William Shakespeare through Friedrich Schiller to Anton Chekhov, Bertolt Brecht, and even to Eugène Ionesco. His works of the 2000s are largely divided into the modern inheritance of the Korean theatrical tradition, the dramatization of figures in Korean history, and the reconstitution of Western masterpieces into Korean theater.

The Eclipse of 2000 is a musical inspired by ancient Korean music and sheds new light on the crises and chaos in modern Korea and the potential for its salvation, which failed to achieve critical acclaim due to its excessively meta-fictional discourse and exaggerated ideality. *The Rural Scholar Cho Nammyung* (2001) represents the righteous and intellectual life of the scholar Cho Sik (1501-1572), well-known as Nammyung by his nom de plume, who is disregarded from public office in central government during the mid-Joseon period. The play

The Rural Scholar Cho Nammyung directed by Lee Youn-taek, 2001
(Photo © Theatre Troupe Georipae)

offered a realistic view on the way in which the aristocratic *yangban* class in Joseon period balanced their scholarly pursuits with physical discipline as evident from their daily routines. Furthermore, the production drew attention to aspects of the *yangban* culture such as *yangbanchum*[49] and *sijochang*,[50] for demonstrating the potential of such cultural assets to continue the tradition as a form of stage performance or a uniquely Korean method of acting.

Written by Lee Youn-taek and directed by Nam Mi-jeong, *A Beautiful Man* embodies elements of universality in using the *chang*, movements, and music of the period in portraying the conflicts between religion and reality faced by Buddhist monks as intellectuals in the martial era of Goryeo Dynasty (918-1392) and their potential for salvation, which successfully evoked poetic appreciation in today's sensibilities. Two other works of historical adaptation, *Dreaming at the Hwaseong Fortress* and *Yi Sun-shin*, also won favorable responses for new interpretations, using the form of popular musicals to portray King Jeongjo (r. 1776-1800), a Joseon-era reformist, and a human perspective to examine Admiral Yi Sun-shin (1545-1598), the legendary military leader who repelled Japan's invasion at sea. Furthermore, *Gungri* (*Clarification of Reason*) dramatizes the life and concerns of a Joseon-era scientist who struggles with the limitation of his lowly social class; and *Crown Princess Hong*, which dramatizes the pain and regrets in the life of a royal lady who, as the mother of King Jeongjo, had to endure the miserable death of her husband.

While working on dramatizing intellectuals and controversial figures in Korean history, Lee was consistent in adapting or newly directing Western classics through his

Yi Sun-shin directed by Lee Youn-taek, 2008 (Photo © Theatre Troupe Georipae)

own perspective. Depicting the titular group of robbers in Schiller's *The Robbers* in 2005, Lee introduced the traditional performing art of *talchum*, while in his 2006 adaptation of Brecht's *Mutter Courage und ihre Kinder* (*Mother Courage and Her Children*), although maintaining the original's plot, Lee changed the identity of Mother Courage from a common vendor to that of a shaman, imbuing a new dimension to the depth and breadth with which the character sees and interprets the fictional universe. At the same time, the timely and contextually appropriate use of *chang* and *pansori* unveiled a new aspect of Brecht's alienation effect. In particular, the actress Kim Mi-suk's outstanding capability and composed performance were effective in emphasizing the stylishness of Korean tradition, while creating an element of the alienation effect to place distance in relation to her character.

Gungri directed by Lee Youn-taek, 2012 (Photo © National Theater Company of Korea, Theatre Troupe Georipae)

Three Sisters directed by Lee Youn-taek, 2008
(Photo © Uri Theatre Institute, Theatre Troupe Georipae)

The Lesson directed by Lee Youn-taek, 2002
(Photo © Uri Theatre Institute, Theatre Troupe Georipae)

Through Chekhov's *Three Sisters*, Lee created characters with clearer and stronger personalities than the original, while highlighting the complex and contradictory aspect of life. Adapting Ionesco's *The Lesson*, Lee reinterpreted the scene in which a professor kills his female student as a murder ritual, by directing the character of the professor to depict the transcendence and madness of a shaman who is possessed by a spirit, and tried to expose the unfathomable and demonic aspects of life at the end of the play by implicitly revealing sexual relations between the professor and his maid.

A work focusing on the use of physicality and materiality, Lee's adaptation of *Hamlet* has continued to be staged since the 1990s, albeit with evolving interpretations. In his production, death generally becomes foregrounded notion: In the last scene of *Hamlet*, all dead bodies return to life and stand up, while the reanimated Hamlet walks upstage towards the white sheets with his naked back towards the audience, creating a powerful image. Keenly interested in acting techniques, Lee argued that as performers inhale, the breath of air must be stored in the pelvis to be exhaled along with the performer's thoughts and feelings in order to stabilize and energize the acting and to imbue the delivery of the play's content with animation. His reinterpretations of *The Robbers*, *The Lesson*, and *Hamlet* were evaluated favorably and received invitations to stages in foreign countries, such as Germany and Romania.

Yang Jeong-woong: A Traveler of the Global Age

Yang Jeong-woong, whose theatrical career began in his 30s during the 2000s, is different from others in many aspects. Before settling down in Korea, Yang spent years with a multinational theater company based in Europe, visiting various countries and participating in the production of plays. Even now, he divides his time between overseas performances and promoting exchanges between theater groups across the world. Among the young theatrical talent to emerge after the 1990s, he holds the rare distinction of actively accepting Korea's culture of traditional entertainment. Therefore, unlike Oh Tae-suk and Lee Youn-taek, Yang's work to modernize traditional Korean entertainment presupposes exchanges and communication with foreign theater to an extent. In this sense, his work is of a similar nature with Kim Jeong-ok at the Jayu Theater Company of the 1980s.

As a member of the Lasenkan International Theatre, Yang performed plays in Spain, India, and Japan, and returned to Korea in 1997 to establish the Yohangza Theatre Company, which was named after the Korean word for "traveler." His early work aimed towards the theatrical depiction of rituals and rites of passage within a cosmopolitan context. Yang first achieved popular recognition for *The Daughter of the Earth*, a physical work of original drama as the result of collaborative creation, which he organized and directed. Premiering in the cave-like space of a small-scale theater, the play caused a sensation with its exotic elegance for utilizing non-linguistic and collective physical expression and creating various images through the sole use of the body, in order to depict a broad spectrum of scenes titled "Matriarchal Society," "Birth," "Song," "A Brave New World," "Propaganda," "Violence," "Sacrifice," "The Cave," and "Blood Marriage." Written and directed by Yang in 2002, *Relation-Karma* is similar in nature, as the play features the modernist recreation of the rite of passage as a tradition ubiquitous among mankind, and although its content was somewhat abstract and subtle, the profound and universal message was embodied in beautiful body language and imagery. This play earned him the award for Best Production at the 2003 Cairo International Festival for Experimental Theatre.

The year 2002 marked changes and robust improvements in Yang's oeuvres through the adaptation of *A Midsummer Night's Dream* into a Korean-style play. Though largely faithful to the original plot, this play replaced the fairies in the original with the *dokkaebi* (goblin) from traditional Korean folklore, and set an old porcine lady Ajumi instead of the original character of Nick Bottom, while Yang virtually rewrote the script to fit Korean-style poetic meter. Accordingly, the performance is naturally filled with motions, rhythms, and sentiments unique to Korea, as well as Korean-style costumes and movements, on-stage colors, and musical accompaniments. Adorned with

A Midsummer Night's Dream directed by Yang Jeong-woong, 2010
(Photo © Theater Company Yohangza)

white face paint and oriental designs, performers made for
a play abundant in energy, rhythm and humor, physically
surpassing the original by running, leaping, and rolling as the
performance demanded. Starting from performances in Tokyo
and at the Edinburgh Fringe Festival, the play was invited
and staged at the Sydney Festival, as well as the Gdansk
Shakespeare Festival in Poland. It was also invited to perform

in Britain at the Barbican Center in 2006 and at Shakespeare's Globe in 2012, winning a favorable response from the audience and critics alike. In particular, the introduction of Korean martial arts invited boisterous laughter and applause from the audience during scenes such as when an unfaithful male *dokkaebi* (originally Titania, a fairy queen) falls in love with an old porcine lady, or when the four lovers chase each other amidst the Athenian woods.

Yang's adaptation of *The Twelfth Night* premiered in 2008 and introduced the concept and performance practices of a *namsadang*, a male-only vagabond troupe in traditional Korean theater, which corresponds with the fact that Shakespeare's plays were only performed by male actors at the time, all the while deepening the layers of amusement in the subject of gender switching, and animating the simple stage with a beautiful traditional color scheme. In 2009's *Hamlet*, Yang actively and boldly introduced the form of Korea's traditional shaman ritual, *gut*. As scenes from the original such as the appearance of the ghost, Ophelia's descent into madness, and Hamlet's death are translated into *gut*, the whole text of *Hamlet* is captured in the formal frame of *gut*, which aims to appease and console the spirit of the dead, in order to guide them to a peaceful afterlife. The performance develops through the symbolic use of large pieces of cloth, thereby emphasizing the Eastern themes of omission, blankness, and transcendence.

The Twelfth Night directed by Yang Jeong-woong, 2009 (Photo © Theater Company Yohangza)

Yang purportedly dreams of staging all of Shakespeare's works as interpretations in the Korean fashion. As the interests in traditional theater and in the globalization of Korean theater as pioneered by Kim Jeong-ok in the 1980s have diminished by a considerable degree, such a lofty aim has only been apparent in the works of Oh Tae-suk, Lee Youn-taek, Yang Jeong-woong, and a few more directors, who are quite conscious of staging on foreign stages. Although "Korean theater based on the Korean tradition of theatrical performance" remains a

Hamlet directed by Yang Jeong-woong, 2009 (Photo © Theater Company Yohangza)

relevant keyword, it is no longer a catchphrase for all. Indeed, what does a "Korean-style performance" signify in this day and age? Does it introduce elements of traditional performing arts? Or does it result from consciousness towards the West as the "Other"? Is it not the case that every theater produced by a Korean is Korean in nature? In order to create the concept of the "Korean theater" to better communicate with world theater of the globalized era, Korean theater must answer an array of existential questions directed at itself.

06

Epilogue

Having begun in the 2000s with the advent of the neoliberal economy, ubiquitous proliferation of digital culture, the advancement of information and communication technology, and the rising popularity of overseas tourism, the universal trend of globalization and its influences have not bypassed the theatrical domain. Since the 1997 International Theater Festival was first held in Seoul, Seoul and other cities have continued to host a variety of international theater festivals of significant scale, thus introducing a number of controversial works by foreign directors including Robert Wilson, Ariane Mnouchkine, Robert Lepage, Eimuntas Nekrošius, and Oskaras Koršunovas within the timeframe of merely several years. Furthermore, as mentioned previously, Korean playwright-directors such as Oh Tae-suk, Lee Youn-taek, Han Tae-sook, Chae Seung-hun, and Yang Jeong-woong have participated in overseas theater festivals both voluntarily and by invitation, thereby showcasing their plays and non-verbal performances on the global stage. Despite the growing complexity of Korea-Japan relations, cultural exchanges with Japan has continued to blossom, bridging the gap between Korea and its close, but distant neighbor. As the scale and international reputation of Seoul's global theater events maintained the rapid pace of advancement, this trend was closely followed by the enhancement of the standard of appreciation among theater audiences in Korea, which is primarily comprised of students. In line with such achievements in Korean theater, the Korea Association of Theatre Critics has played an active role since the 2000s as the competent branch of the International Association of Theatre Critics.

As a widespread trend across the world, original drama of noteworthy quality have been rare to emerge, while the passion of diverse efforts to deconstruct classical theater such as Shakespeare or Chekhov has persevered. If the reinterpretation and deconstruction of Shakespeare by prominent contemporary directors had begun in the 1990s, the 2000s saw the work of Anton Chekhov also gain similar contemporary dedication. While Chekhov's works directed by Lev Dodin, Kama Ginkas, and Yury Butusov were introduced to Korea, a variety of Chekhov's plays were also reinterpreted and staged by Korean directors including Lee Seong-yeol, Yun Gwang-jin, Lee Youn-taek, Im Do-wan, and Seong Gi-wung. While Lee Seong-yeol translated Chekhov into the form of a mime, Im Do-wan and Seong Gi-wung set the background of their Chekhov adaptations as Korea under Japanese colonial rule. More recent efforts in Korean theatrical circles have included the deconstruction of modern playwrights such as Arthur Miller and August Strindberg, notable among which is Kim Hyeon-tak's deconstruction of *Death of a Salesman*, which takes place on a single treadmill. Furthermore, a rising number of young theater artists continue to extend the boundaries of theater by staging non-verbal or multimedia performances that transcends the confines of particular genres.

This book does not make any separate commentary dedicated to musicals. History of the Korean musical scene began in the 1960s as a small number of original foreign musicals were imported to the Korean stage, paving the way for the 1980s and the emergence of commercial theater, which introduced unaltered adaptations of West End and Broadway musicals including *Jesus Christ Super Star*, *The Sound of Music*, and *Guys and Dolls*. With the propagation of consumerist culture in the 1990s, directly imported or licensed foreign musicals attracted greater audiences. Significantly raising the bar for Korean musicals, *The Last Empress*, which was produced by Acom and directed by Yun Ho-jin in 1995, was an astounding achievement in reaching Broadway in the U.S. In the 2000s, the quality and technologies of the musical industry highly improved, and Park Myung-sung's Seensee Company, which grew by staging licensed musicals, drew attention with a large-scale collaboration with foreign professionals to produce an original musical titled *Dancing*

Shadows.[51] As the market continues to grow, the rise of renowned musical stars attract loyal fans both in original and licensed musicals and not only in Korea but also in Japan, and the art form of the musical is fast becoming a thriving sector in the Korean entertainment industry.

This book also does not discuss public theaters such as national, municipal, and provincial theaters. Founded in 1950, the National Theater Company of Korea struggled with the immediate onset of war after its launch and yet made contributions to developing the theatrical scene with productions of realistic plays centering on the National Theater of Korea in Myeong-dong until the mid-1960s. After relocating to a new building situated around Mt. Namsan in 1973, the reality of military dictatorship resulted in a restrictive environment for the theater company until the end of 1980s; during this time, the National Theater Company was unable to produce progressive and creative original drama, and instead, focused on introducing large-scale Western classics, which were difficult for private theater companies to stage. Recently, the theater company has separated from being an affiliate of the National Theater of Korea in Mt. Namsan and once again relocated to a new theater building behind the Seoul Station, and it has since dedicated its efforts to discovering a new form of contemporary theater incorporating elements of Korean identity and values.

Since the 2010s, public theaters under government budget

have begun to participate in theater productions and take the lead in the theatrical world. For example, along with the National Theater Company of Korea, such producing theaters based in Seoul include Myeongdong Theater, Seoul Arts Center, and Namsan Arts Center. As of 2014, current problems facing the theatrical scene in Korea are its bipolarization and the attenuation of small-scale original theater produced by private theater groups. Bipolarization is a deepening trend: Whereas audiences still gather to see foreign works of outstanding mise-en-scène that are invited to Korea for international theater festivals, flamboyant works of licensed musicals, and performances by relatively well-funded public theaters, small-scale and serious plays by ordinary theater companies, which subsist through grants from the Arts Council Korea (ARKO), tend to suffer from the problem of bipolarization as they often fail to maintain a standard of artistic integrity and struggle to find an audience outside of a small number of students.

Notes

1   Another reason is that the preceding publication by Kim Miy He mainly deals with the 1960s when adaptations of American and European plays were widely introduced in Korea. However, certain works on Korean theater include the 1960s in the examination of contemporary theater.

2   The term *gilnori* or *apnori* refers to the beginning entertainment to arouse excitement.

3   The term *yangban* refers to the aristocracy during the Joseon era (1392-1897).

4   A Korean-style drum, with a drumhead on each of the two sides and played with a single wooden stick.

5   The term *gosu* refers to the percussionist.

6   *Changgeuk* is a modern version of *pansori*, and a theater form that emerged in Korea from the early 20th century. The performance consists of singers and performers assuming the roles of several characters, while appearing on stage simultaneously, reproducing *pansori* or other romantic stories in a mix of elements of reality and glamorous spectacles. The format of *changgeuk* remains without solid affirmation, and various stylistic experiments continue to date.

7   The literal meaning of *shimpa* refers to "new wave" in contrast to traditional Japanese theater *gupa* ("old wave," e.g. *noh, kabuki*). *Shimpa* is an early-modern form of theater comprised of realistic and melodramatic elements added to the *gupa* format. During the Japanese occupation, *shimpa* exerted an enormous influence on Korean theater; it is viewed by some as having served as the foundational basis prior to realistic theater in both countries.

8   Originally titled *Daljip* in Korean, which refers to heaps of straw that are

burned in a ritual to drive away evil spirits to usher in the spring in rural areas.

9   At present, Korean TV dramas are exported widely around the world, including Japan, China, Southeast Asia, the Middle East, and South America, generating a boom in Korean popular culture and gaining widespread popularity. The nature of the sudden popularity of Korean culture, or *hallyu*, is a major subject in dramaturgical studies.

10   The original architect of the Drama Center remains unidentified. Some say that Yu Chi-jin presented the idea after visiting theatrical facilities around the world; while others claim that it was the work of Kim Jung-eop, a well-known architect of the time.

11   *Chobun* refers to tomb made of dry grass, to store and dry the corpse after funerary rituals.

12   A cleansing ritual for the living, aimed to help guide them to a better place after death.

13   Suk-hyeon Kim, *Directors of the Drama Center*, p. 98, Seoul: Hyundai Meehak Press, 2005.

14   Korean classical music played in the royal court.

15   *Sijo* refers to Korean poetic form generally recited by the aristocratic *yangban* class.

16   *Gok* refers to the wailing as the expression of sadness for the dead at a traditional Korean funeral.

17   Suk-hyeon Kim, *op. cit.*, p. 255.

18   *Jinogwi-gut* refers to shamanic rituals held to guide the dead to the underworld paradise.

19   The three goblins symbolize factors of hardship for farmers such as imported crops, water damage by typhoons and floods, and the tenant-farming system.

20   Bang Ock Kim, "Study on *Madanggeuk*," *Aesthetics of Open Theater*, p. 130, Seoul: Munyemadang, 1997.

21   Hyun-min Kim, *The Study of Madanggeuk of the 1970s*, Ewha Womans University Master's Thesis Majoring in Korean Language & Literature, 1993, p. 32.

22   *Mudang* refers to Korean shamans, typically women, who host shamanic rituals.

23   In *Nolbudyeon*, Choi In-hoon attempted to restructure the famous Korean classical story of *Heungbujeon*, featuring the greedy elder brother Nolbu and the kind younger brother Heungbu.

24   Sang-cheol Han, "De-aestheticization of *Madanggeuk*," *Issues and Reflections in Korean Theater*, p. 155, Hyundai Meehak Press, 1992.

25   Bang Ock Kim, *op. cit.*, "Study on *Madanggeuk*"

26   Min-yeong Yu, "Allegorical Conversation on Contemporary History," *Art and Criticism*, 1986, Spring, p. 318.

27   Hae-suk Yang, "Discussion on Oh Tae-suk," *Discussion of Active Korean Playwrights 2*. Seoul: Edited by Korean Association of Theater Critics.

28   Sang-cheol Han, "Exploration of Korean Identity," *Moonlight over the Baekma River* (Compilation of Oh Tae-suk's Plays 5), p. 294, Seoul: Pyungmin Press.

29   *Jangseung* are sculptures in the shape of a man and a woman, usually erected near the entrance of a village for the sake of its spiritual protection.

30   Sang-cheol Han, "Flowers Bloom on the Windy Day," *Monthly Music Performing Arts Magazine Auditorium*, January 1985.

31   "After Viewing *Flowers Bloom on the Windy Day*," *The Mainichi Newspapers*, June 1985.

32   Sang-cheol Han, "Sad Songs of Clowns," *Hankookilbo*, February 21, 1984.

33   Hyeon-suk Shin, *Western Dramas in Korea*, p. 100, Seoul: Sohwa Press, 1999, 100.

34   Jong-wu Kim, *Study of History of Hamlet Staged by Ki Kook-seo*. Seoul: Chung-Ang University Department of Theater Master's Thesis, 2002.

35   *Heojaebi* can either refer to a scarecrow or a puppet.

36   A transcendental being in Buddhism said to appear when the masses face insurmountable hardships.

37   Se-gon Oh, "Chae Seung-hun: Pioneering Korean Avant-garde Theater," *Study of Korean Modern Directors I*, p. 226, Seoul: Theatre and Man Press, 2012.

38   *Ibid.*, p. 227.

39   ZakEunShinHwa, literally meaning a "little myth."

40   Seong-hui Kim, "The Theory of Cho Kwang-hwa," *Aesthetics of Korean Theater and Daily Lives*, p. 151, Seoul: Theatre and Man Press, 2009.

41   Traditional Korean martial arts involving kicks and leg hooks to dislodge the opponent.

42   Also known as *subak*, traditional Korean martial arts emphasizing hand-to-hand attacks and self-discipline.

43   Bang Ock Kim, "Highlighting the Life and Ideals that Transcend Time and Space," *Dong-A Ilbo*, July 4, 1991.

44   An all-male troupe of vagabond theater which wandered through the country, entertaining the masses with a repertoire consisting of music, dance, short mask performances, and acrobatics.

45   A biography of a man named Jugong.

46   The name of a village.

47   The name of a region in Korea.

48   The name of a village in Korea.

49   Courtly dance favored among Joseon's aristocratic *yangban* class.

50   Melodious poetry recited by the *yangban*.

51   Ariel Dorfman's adaptation of Cha Beom-seok's original *Sanbul*.

Bibliography

An, Chi-un, *Performing Arts and Practical Criticism*. Seoul: Moonji Publishing, 1993.

Compilation Committee of Korean Modern Theater (ed.), *A Century of Modern Theater in Korea*. Seoul: Jipmoondang, 2009.

Han, Sang-cheol, *Issues and Reflections in Korean Theater*. Seoul: Hyundai Meehak Press, 1992.

Kim, Ah-jeong & Graves, R.B. (ed. and trans.), *The Multicultural Theatre of Oh Tae-suk: Five Plays from Korean Avant-Garde*. University of Hawaii Press, 1999.

Kim, Bang Ock, *A Medicine Seller, Agnes of God, and Madanggeuk: The Korean Theater in a Turbulent Era*. Seoul: Moonumsa, 1989.

_____, *Opening the 21st Century with Theater: Body, Deconstruction, Performance*. Seoul: Theatre and Man Press, 2003.

Kim, Hyun-min, *The Study of Madanggeuk of the 1970s*. Seoul: Ewha Womans University Master's Thesis Majoring in Korean Language & Literature, 1993.

Kim, Jong-wu, *Study of History of Hamlet Staged by Ki Kook-seo*. Seoul: Chung-Ang University Department of Theater Master's Thesis, 2002.

Kim, Mi-do, *The Korean Theater in the End of a Century*. Seoul: Taehaksa, 1998.

Kim, Miy He, *Acts and Scenes: Western Drama in Korean Theater*. Seoul: Hollym Corp., Publishers, 2013.

Kim, Seong-hui, *Aesthetics of Korean Theater and Daily Lives*. Seoul: Theatre and Man Press, 2009.

Kim, Suk-hyeon, *Directors of the Drama Center*. Seoul: Hyundai Meehak Press, 2005.

Kim, Yun-cheol (ed.) *Contemporary Korean Theatre: Playwrights, Directors, Stage-Designers*. Seoul: Theatre and Man Press, 2000.

Korean Theater Studies Association (ed.), *The Study of Modern Directors in Korea 1, 2*. Seoul: Theatre and Man Press, 2012.

Lee, Chin A, *Daehangno: Theater District in Seoul*. Seoul: Hollym Corp., Publishers, 2013.

Lee, Hyon-U (ed.), *Glocalizing Shakespeare and Beyond*. Seoul: Dongin Publishing, 2009.

Lee Mi-won, *Postmodernist Era and the Korean Theater*. Seoul: Hyundai Meehak Press, 1996.

Seo, Yeon-ho & Lee, Sang-wu, *100 Years of Korean Theater*. Seoul: Hyeonamsa, 2000.

Yu, Min-yeong, *The History of Modern Theater in Korea*. Seoul: Dankook University Press, 1996.